Edward Stillingfleet

The Doctrines and Practices of the Church of Rome Truly Represented

in answer to a book intituled, A Papist misrepresented, and represented

Edward Stillingfleet

The Doctrines and Practices of the Church of Rome Truly Represented
in answer to a book intituled, A Papist misrepresented, and represented

ISBN/EAN: 9783337381141

Printed in Europe, USA, Canada, Australia, Japan

Cover: Foto ©Lupo / pixelio.de

More available books at **www.hansebooks.com**

THE DOCTRINES AND PRACTICES OF THE Church of Rome

TRULY REPRESENTED;

In Answer to a Book Intituled,

A Papist Misrepresented, and Represented, &c.

The Third Edition Corrected.

LONDON:
Printed for *W. Rogers*, at the Sun over against St. *Dunstan's* Church in *Fleetstreet*. 1686.

The Doctrine and Practices of the Church of *Rome*, truly Represented, &c.

An Answer to the Introduction.

THE *Introduction* consists of two parts,

I. A general Complaint of the *Papists* being *Misrepresented* among us.
II. An Account of the Method he hath taken to clear them from these *Misrepresentations*.

I. As to the *First*; Whether it be just, or not, must be examin'd in the several Particulars. But here we must consider, whether it serves the End it is designed for in this place, which is, to gain the Reader's good Opinion of their Innocency: Not meerly because they complain so much of being injured, but because the best Men in all Times have been *misrepresented*; as he proves at large in this *Introduction*, from several Examples of the Old and New *Testament, but especially of Christ and his Apostles, and the Primitive Christians.* But it is observable, that when Bp *Jewel* began his excellent *Apology* for the *Church of England*, with a Complaint much of the same Nature, and produced the very same Examples, his Adversary would by no means allow it to have any Force, being, as he called it, *Exordium Commune*, which might be used on both sides, and therefore could be proper to neither. And although it be reasonable only for those to complain of being *misrepresented*, who having Truth on their side, do notwithstanding suffer under the Imputation of Error; yet it is possible for those who are very much *mistaken*, to complain of being *misrepresented*; and while they

they go about to remove the Misrepresentations of others, to make new Ones of their own. And as the best Men, and the best Things, have been misrepresented; so other Men have been as apt to complain of it; and the worst Things are as much misrepresented, when they are made to appear not so bad as they are. For *Evil* is as truly misrepresented under the appearance of *Good*, as *Good* under the appearance of *Evil*; and it is hard to determine whether hath done the greater Mischief.

So that if *the Father of Lies be the Author of Misrepresenting*, (as the *Introduction* begins) we must have a care of him both ways. For when *he tried this black Art in Paradise*, (as our Author speaks) it was both by misrepresenting the Command, and the Danger of transgressing it. He did not only make the Command appear otherwise than it was; but he did very much lessen the Punishment of Disobedience, and by that means deluded our first Parents into that Sin and Misery, under which their Posterity still suffers. Which ought to be a Caution to them, how dangerous it is to break the Law of God under the fairest Colour and Pretences; and that they should not be easily imposed upon by false Glosses, and plausible Representations, though made by such as therein pretend to be *Angels of Light*.

But although *the Father of Lies be the Author of Misrepresenting*: yet we have no reason to think, but that if he were to plead his own Cause to Mankind, he would very much complain of being *misrepresented* by them; and even in this respect, when they make him the *Father* of those *Lies* which are their own Inventions. And can that be a certain Argument of Truth, which may as well be used by *the Father of Lies*?

And the great Instruments he hath made use of in deceiving and corrupting Mankind, have been as forward as any to complain of being *misrepresented*. The true Reason is, Because no great Evil can prevail in the World, unless it be represented otherwise than it is; and all Men are not competent Judges of the Colours of Good and Evil; therefore when the Designs of those who go about to deceive, begin to be laid open, they then betake themselves to the fairest Representations they can make of themselves, and hope that many will not see through their Pretences.

If

If I had a mind to follow our Author's Method, I could make as long a Deduction of Instances of this kind. But I shall content my self with some few Examples of those who are allowed on both sides to have been guilty of great Errors and Corruptions.

The *Arrians* pleaded they were *misrepresented*, when they were taken for Enemies to Christ's Divinity; for all that they contended for, was only such a Moment of Time, as would make good the Relation between Father and Son.

The *Pelagians*, with great Success for some time (and even at *Rome*) complained that they were very much *misrepresented*, as Enemies to God's Grace; whereas they owned and asserted the manifold Grace of God; and were only Enemies to Mens Idleness, and neglect of their Duties.

The *Nestorians* gave out, that they never intended to make two Persons in Christ, as their Adversaries charged them; but all their design was to avoid Blasphemy, in calling the Blessed Virgin *the Mother of God*; and whatever went beyond this, was their Adversaries *Misrepresentations*, and not their own Opinions.

The *Eutychians* thought themselves very hardly dealt with, for saying, there was *but one Nature in Christ*; they did not mean thereby (as they said) to destroy the Properties of the Humane Nature, but only to assert that its Subsistence was swallowed up by the Divine; and of all Persons, those have no reason to blame them, who suppose the Properties of one Substance may be united to another.

Even the *Gentile Idolaters*, when they were charged by the Christians, *that they worshipped Stocks and Stones*, complained, they were *misrepresented*; for they were not such Ideots, to take things for Gods, which had neither Life, nor Sense, nor Motion in them. And when they were charged *with worshipping other Gods as they did the Supream*; they desired their Sense might not be taken from common Prejudices, or vulgar Practices, but from the Doctrine of their Philosophers; and they owned a Soveraign Worship due to him that was Chief; and a subordinate and Relative to some Cœlestial Beings, whom they made Application to as Mediators between him and them. Must all these Complaints now be taken for granted? what then becomes of the Reputation of General Councils, or the Primitive Christians? But as, if it were enough to be Accused, none would be Innocent; so none would be Guilty, if it were enough to complain of being *misrepresented*.

Therefore in all Complaints of this Nature, it is necessary to come to Particulars; and to examine with Care and Diligence the Matters complained of, and then to give Judgment in the *Case*. I am glad to find our Author professing so much *Sincerity and Truth without Passion*; and I do assure him I shall follow what he professes: For the Cause of our Church is such, as needs neither Tricks nor Passion to defend it; and therefore I shall endeavour to state the Matters in Difference, with all the clearness and calmness that may be; and I shall keep close to his Method and Representations, without Digressions, or provoking Reflections.

II. But I must declare my self very much unsatisfied with the Method he hath taken to clear his Party from these *Misrepresentations*. For,

1. He takes upon him to draw a double Character of a Papist; and in the one he pretends to follow a certain Rule, but not in the other; which is not fair and ingenuous.

As to the one, he saith, *He follows the Council of* Trent, *and their allowed Spiritual Books and Catechisms*: and we find no fault with this. But why must the other Part then be drawn by Fancy, or common Prejudices, or ignorant Mistakes? Have we no Rule, whereby the Judgment of our Church is to be taken? Are not our Articles as easy to be had and understood, as the Decrees and Canons of the Council of *Trent*? I will not ask, How the Council of *Trent* comes to be the Rule and Measure of Doctrine to any here, where it was never received? But I hope I may, why our Representations are not to be taken from the Sense of our Church, as their's from the Council of *Trent*? If he saith, *his Design was to remove common Prejudices, and vulgar Mistakes*; it is easy to answer, if they are contrary to the Doctrine of our Church, we utterly disown them. We know very well there are Persons, who have so false a Notion of *Popery*, that they charge the Rites and Customs of our Church with it: but we pity their Weakness and Folly, and are far from defending such Misrepresentations. But that which we adhere to, is the Doctrine and Sense of our

Church,

Church, as it is by Law established; and what Representations are made agreeable thereto, I undertake to defend, and no other. But if a Person take the liberty to lay on what Colours he pleases on one side, it will be no hard matter to take them off in the other, and then to say, *How much fairer is our Church than she is painted!* It is an easy, but not so allowable a way of disputing, for the same Person to make the Objections and Answers too; for he may so model and frame the Arguments by a little Art, that the Answers may appear very full and sufficient; whereas if they had been truly represented, they would be found very lame and defective.

2. He pretends to give an Account why he quotes no Authors for his Misrepresentations, which is very unsatisfactory, viz. *That he hath described the Papist therein, exactly according to the apprehension he had of him when he was a Protestant.* But how can we tell what sort of Protestant he was; nor how well he was instructed in his Religion? And must the Character now supposed to be common to Protestants, be taken from his ignorant, or childish, or wilful Mistakes? Did ever any Protestant that understands himself, say, *That Papists are never permitted to hear Sermons which they are able to understand?* (p. 58.) Or, *that they held it lawful to commit Idolatry?* (p. 9.) Or, *that a Papist believes the Pope to be his great God, and to be far above all Angels? &c.* Yet these are some of his Misrepresentations, (*pag.* 40.) Did he in earnest think so himself? If he did, he gives no good account of himself: if he did not, he gives a worse; for then how shall we believe him in other things, when he saith, *He hath drawn his Misrepresentations exactly according to his own apprehensions?* It is truth, he saith, *he added some few Points, which were violently charged on him by his Friends:* but we dare be bold to say, these were none of them. But let us suppose it true, that he had such Apprehensions himself. Are these fit to be printed as the Character of a Party? What would they say to us, if a Spanish Convert should give a Character of *Protestants* according to the common Opinion the People there have of them; and set down in one Column their monstrous Misrepresentations,

tations, and in another, what he found them to be since his coming hither; and that in good Truth he saw they were just like other Men? But suppose he had false Apprehensions before he went among them; why did he not take care to inform himself better before he changed? Had he no Friends, no Books, no Means to rectify his Mistakes? Must he needs leave one Church, and go to another, before he understood either? If this be a true Account of himself, it is but a bad Account of the Reasons of his Change.

3. The Account he gives of the other Part of his Character, affords as little Satisfaction: For although in the general, it be well that he pretends to keep to a Rule; yet,

(1.) He shews no Authority he hath to interpret that Rule in his own sense. Now several of his Representations, depend upon his own private Sense and Opinions, against the Doctrine of many others as zealous for their Church as himself; and what reason have we to adhere to his Representations, rather than to theirs? As for instance, he saith, *The Pope's personal Infallibility is no Matter of Faith* (p. 42.) But there are others say it is, and is grounded on the same Promises which makes him Head of the Church. Why now must we take his Representation rather than theirs? And so as to the *Deposing Power*, he grants, *it hath been the Opinion of several Popes* (and Councils too) *but that it is no Matter of Faith,* (p. 47.) But whose Judgment are we to take in this Matter, according to the Principles of their Church? A private Man's, of no Name, no Authority; or of those Popes and Councils who have declared it, and acted by it? And can any Man of their Church justify our relying upon his Word, against the Declaration of Popes and Councils? But suppose the Question be about the Sense of his own Rule, *the Council of Trent:* what Authority hath he to declare it, when the Pope hath expresly forbidden all Prelates to do it, and reserved it to the Apostolical See?

<small>Bulla *Pii 4ti* super Confirmat. Concil. Tridentini.</small>

(2.) He leaves out, in the several Particulars, an essential part of the Character of a *Papist* since the Council of *Trent*;

Trent; which is, that he doth not only believe the Doctrines there defined to be true, but to be necessary to Salvation. And there is not a word of this in his Representation of the Points of Doctrine, but the whole is managed as though there were nothing but a difference about some particular Opinions; whereas in Truth, the Necessity of holding those Doctrines, in order to Salvation, is the main Point in difference. If Men have no mind to believe their own Senses, we know not how to help it; but we think it is very hard to be told, we cannot be saved unless we renounce them too. And this now appears to be the true State of the Case, since *Pius* the 4*th* drew up and published a Confession of Faith, according to the Decrees and Canons of the Council of *Trent*, wherein Men are not only required *to believe their Traditions as firmly as the Bible, the Seven Sacraments, Transubstantiation, the Sacrifice of the Mass, Purgatory, Invocation of Saints, worshipping of Images, Indulgences, Supremacy,* &c. but they must believe, *that without believing these things, there is no Salvation to be had* in the ordinary Way: for after the enumeration of those Points, it follows, *Hanc veram Catholicam fidem extra quàm nemo salvus esse potest,* &c. This is the true *Catholick* Faith, *without which no Man can be saved*; *i. e.* The belief of these things is thereby declared as necessary to Salvation, as of any other Articles of the Creed. But it may be objected, *The subscribing this Profession of Faith, is not required of all Members of that Church.* To which I answer, That to make a Man a Member of it, he must declare that he holds the same Faith which the Church of *Rome* holds: And this is as much the Faith of the Roman Church, as the Pope and Council of *Trent* could make it. And it is now printed in the Roman *Ritual* at *Paris*, set forth by *Paul* the 5*th*, as the Confession of Faith owned by the Church of *Rome*. And therefore this ought to have been a part of the true Representation, as to the Doctrinal Points; but when he comes to the 35*th* Head, he then owns, *That unless Men do believe every Article of the Roman Faith, they cannot be saved*, (p. 96.) *and he that disbelieves one, does in a manner disbelieve all,* (p. 97.) Which may as well reach those who disown

B 2 the

the Depofing Power, and the Pope's perfonal Infallibility, as Us, fince thofe are accounted Articles of Faith by the ruling part of their Church, to whom it chiefly belongs to declare them; and the former hath been defined both by Popes and Councils.

(3.) He never fets down what it is which makes any Doctrine to become a Doctrine of their Church. We are often blamed for charging particular Opinions upon their Church: but we defire to know what it is which makes a Doctrine of their Church; *i.e.* whether frequent and publick Declaration, by the Heads and Guides of their Church, be fufficient or not to that End? Our Author feems to imply the Neceffity of fome Conditions to be obferved; for befides *the Pope's Authority*, he requires *due Circumftances, and proceeding according to Law*, (p. 42.) But who is to be Judg of thefe Circumftances and legal Proceeding? And he never tells what thefe *Circumftances* are. And yet after all, he faith, *The Orders of the Supream Paftor are to be obey'd, whether he be infallible or not.* And this now brings the Matter home; *The Popes*, he confeffes, *have owned the Depofing Doctrine, and acted according to it:* And others are bound to obey their Orders, whether infallible or not; and confequently they are bound by the Doctrine of their Church to act, when the Popes fhall require it, according to the Depofing Power. But he feems to fay, in this Cafe, that a Doctrine of their Church is to be judged by the Number; for, faith he, *There are greater Numbers that difown this Doctrine*, (p. 47.) I will not at prefent difpute it; but I defire to be informed, Whether the Doctrines of their Church go by majority of Votes, or not? I had thought the Authority of the Guides of the Church, ought to have over-ballanced any Number of Diffenters. For, what are thofe who refufe to fubmit to the Dictates of Popes and Councils, but Diffenters from the Church of *Rome*? The diftinction of the *Court and Church of Rome*, is wholly impertinent in this Cafe. For, we here confider not the meer Temporal Power which makes the Court, but the Spiritual Capacity of Teaching the Church: and if Popes and Councils may err in Teaching this Doctrine, why not in any other? I know there are some that say, *Universal Tradition is necessary to make a Doctrine of their Church*. But then no submission can be required to any Doctrine in that Church, till the Universal Tradition of it, in all Times, and in all Parts of the Christian Church, be proved. And we need to desire no better Terms than these, as to all Points of Pope *Pius* the 4th his Creed, which are in dispute between us and them.

(4.) He makes use of the Authority of some particular Divines, as delivering the Sense of their Church, when there are so many of greater Authority against them. Whereas, if we proceed by his own Rule, the greater Number is to carry it. Therefore we cannot be thought to *misrepresent* them, if we charge them with such things as are owned, either by the general and allowed Practices of their Church, or their Publick Offices, or the generality of their Divines and Casuists; or in case of a Contest, with that side which is owned by the Guides of their Church, when the other is censured; or which was approved by their Canonized Saints, or declared by their Popes and Councils, whose Decrees they are bound to follow. And by these Measures I intend to proceed, having no design to *misrepresent them*, as indeed we need not.

And so much in Answer to the *Introduction*.

I. *Of Praying to Images.*

IN this, and the other Particulars, where it is neceſſary, I ſhall obſerve this Method;

1. To give a clear and impartial Account of the State of the Controverſy in as few Words as I can.

2. To make ſome Reflections on what he ſaith, in order to the clearing them from Miſrepreſentations.

As to the State of the Controverſy, as it ſtands, ſince the Council of *Trent*, we are to conſider.

1. We muſt diſtinguiſh between what Perſons do in their own Opinion, and what they do according to the Senſe of the Divine Law. It is poſſible that Men may intend one thing, and the Law give another Senſe of it: as is often ſeen in the Caſe of Treaſon; although the Perſons plead never ſo much they had no intention to commit Treaſon; yet if the Law makes their Act to be ſo, their diſavowing it doth not excuſe them. So it is in the preſent Caſe; Men may have real and ſerious Intentions, to refer their final, ultimate, and Soveraign Worſhip only to God; but if the Law of God ſtrictly and ſeverely prohibits this particular Manner of Worſhip by Images, in as full, plain, and clear Words as may be, and gives a Denomination to ſuch Acts, taken from the immediate Object of it; no particular Intention of the Perſons can alter that Denomination, or make the Guilt to be leſs than the Law makes it.

2. There can be no *Miſrepreſenting* as to the lawfulneſs of many External Acts of Worſhip, with Reſpect to Images, which are owned by them. But it doth not look fairly to put the Title, *Of Praying to Images*; for the Queſtion is, *about the Worſhip of Images:* whereas this Title would inſinuate, as though we did directly charge them with *Praying to their Images, without any farther Reſpect.* Which we are ſo far from charging them with, that I do not know of any People in the World, who are not like *Stones and Stocks* them-

themselves, who are liable to that Charge. The *PEN-DETS*, in the *East-Indies* are fully cleared from it, by *Thevenot*, as well as *Bernier*. And it would be hard we should not allow the same to our Fellow-Christians. I do therefore grant what our Author saith, *viz. That all the Veneration they express before Images, whether by kneeling, praying, lifting up the Eyes, burning Candles, Incense,* &c. *is not at all done for the Image, but is wholly referr'd to the things represented, which he intends to honour by these Actions.* But I hope now, it is no Misrepresenting for us to say, that *they do kneel, pray, lift up their Eyes, burn Candles, Incense,* &c. *before their Images*; which is all I charge them with at present.

Thevenot *Voyage des Indes*. p. 188.
Bernier *Memoirs. Tom. 3.* p. 172.
Pag. 3.

3. To perform these Acts before Images, without a design to worship the Images by them, is declared, by great Divines of the Church of *Rome*, to be next to Heresy. The Case was this; There were before the Council of *Trent*, several Persons who lived in Communion of that Church, but by no means approved the Worship of Images, such as *Durandus, Holcot, Picus Mirandula*, and others. Now these Persons thought fit to comply in these External Acts, but declared they intended not to worship the Images, but the Objects before them. Since the Council of *Trent* decreed Images were to be worshipped, this Case hath been debated by the Divines and Casuists of greatest Reputation among them; And *Suarez* saith, *This way of Durandus is dangerous, rash, and savours of Heresy*: and he saith further from *Medina, That it was* Victoria's *Opinion, that it was Heretical*; but he adds, that his own Opinion, *that Images were truly and properly to be Worshipped, was generally received by their Divines*: and therefore I need name no more.

Suarez *in 3. part, Qu. 25. Disp. 53. Sect. 3. 2do. principaliter & Sect. 5.*

4. It is granted by their Divines and Casuists, that the People in the Worship of Images may easily fall into Idolatry.

(1.) If the Worship do not pass from the Image to the Thing represented. And so *Aquinas* himself determines, That no Irrational Creature is capable of Worship, but as it hath Respect to a Rational Being. But here lies the Difficulty,

Difficulty, how an Extrinsecal Relation to an Object of Worship, where the Thing is confessed to deserve none, can give any Reason for its being properly worshipped. But they all grant, if the Worship stop at the Inanimate part, it can be no other than the Worship of Stocks and Stones.

(2.) If the Worship be given to the Image, which is proper to God alone. This *Bellarmin* is forced to grant, because the Evidence is so clear in Antiquity, that the *Gnosticks* were condemned for some Worship which they performed to the Image of Christ. Now, we cannot think that these *Gnosticks* were such Sots, as to take the Image of Christ to be Christ himself; and therefore whatever Worship it was, it must be Relative, *i. e.* given to the Image for the sake of Christ represented by it.

Bellarmin. de Imag. l.2. c. 24.

(3.) *If the People believe any Divinity to be in the Images, or put any Trust or Confidence in them*; then the Council of *Trent* it self owns such to be like the Heathen Idolaters. Now, how shall it be known when the People believe Divinity to be in Images, but by some more than ordinary Presence or Operation in or by them? by their having a greater Opinion of one Image than of another of the same Person? by their going long Pilgrimages to certain Images in hopes of Relief, when they might easily cause Images to represent at home?

Concil. Trident. S.ss. 25.

And that such are no extravagant Imaginations, is known to all who have heard of *Loretto*, or *Compostella*, or other Places nearer home. I need not mention the Complaints of *Polydore Virgil*, *Cassander*, or *Wicelius* to this purpose, who all died in the Communion of the Church of *Rome*; for the same is very lately complained of by a Considerable Person in that Communion, who saith, *The greatest part of the Devotion of the People of* Italy, Spain, *and* Portugal, *consists in prostrating themselves before Images, and going in Pilgrimage to them, and hoping for Remission of their Sins by so doing.* And another very lately yields, *That to avoid the peril of Idolatry, to which* (he saith) *the People is evidently exposed by the use of Images, it would be necessary to take them away from the Altars, and by no means to have them allowed for the Objects of Religious Worship.*

Moyens Surs & honestes pour la Conversion de tous les Heretiques. To. 2. p. 115.

Entretiens de Philalethe & Philirene. 2d part, p. 157.

The

The Question now is, Whether the Council of *Trent* hath taken any effectual Course to prevent these *Abuses*? If not, what *Misrepresenting* is it to charge the Abuses upon the Doctrines and Practices allowed by it?

The Remedies prescribed by the Council, are these;

1. *Declaring that there is no Divinity or Vertue in them for which they should be worshipped; and that nothing is to be desired of them, nor any Trust or Confidence to be put in them.*

2. *Expressing their earnest desire, that if any Abuses have crept in, they may be removed.*

But in the mean time the Council decrees, *the Images not only to be useful to be set up in Churches, but to have due Honour and Worship given them there, for the sake of those they represent; as not only putting off the Hat, but falling down before them.* And the *Roman Catechism* declares, *That this Worship is very beneficial to the People, and so much is to be told them; and that Images are to be in Churches, not meerly for Instruction, sed ut colantur, that they may be worshipped.* Catechis. Rom. Part. 3. c. 2. §. 14.

But what could the Council do more, than to desire all *Abuses* may be taken away; and is it not then the fault of others, and not of the Council, if they be not?

I grant, the Council doth desire *Abuses* may be taken away, if any such be; but then it enumerates those Abuses; in *Heterodox Images*, in *making Gain of Images*, in painting them too *wantonly*: but besides, it doth say, *that all Superstition be removed in the Sacred Use of Images*; but it doth not say in the *Worship of them*; and so it may relate to *Magick* and *Divination*. But that the Council could not prevent, or design to prevent the *Abuses* mention'd in the Worship of Images, will appear by these things.

1. The Council of *Trent* allows the highest Relative Worship to be given to them; it setting no bounds to it, so it be for the sake of the Prototypes.

2. It allows a Worship to be given to the Images themselves too; for it confirms the second Council of *Nice*, which decreed an inferiour Adoration to be given to them.

3. It disapproves no Customs then practised among them in the Worship of Images; which were all known, and by many complained of, both as Pilgrimages to them, and the carrying of them about in Procession, and the solemn Consecration of them; the Form whereof is not only inserted, but inlarged in the new Pontifical since the Council of *Trent*. And it is to be observed, that in the old Pontifical, *A. D.* 1511. there is no Form for consecrating an Image; in that of *Paul* the 3*d*, it is inserted, but out of *Durandus*; but in that of *Clement* the 8*th*, it is put in more largely, and as authentically as if it had been always there. And is not this the way to reform the Worship of Images?

To come now to our Author's Reflections on the *Misrepresentation* he saith hath been made as to this Point.

1. *A Papist represented, believes it damnable to worship Stocks and Stones for Gods; to pray to Pictures or Images of Christ, the Virgin* Mary, *or any other Saints.*

These Expressions are capable of a double Sense, and therefore this is not fair Representing.

(1.) *To worship Stocks or Stones for Gods*, may signify two things. (1.) To believe the very Stocks and Stones to be Gods. And this we do not charge them with. (2.) To give to Images made of Wood and Stone, the Worship due only to God; and so by construction of the Fact, to make them *Gods*, by giving them *Divine Worship*. And if they will clear themselves of this, they must either prove that *External Adoration* is no part of Divine Worship, (notwithstanding the Scripture makes it so, and all the rest of Mankind look upon it as such, even Jews, Turks, and Infidels;) or that their external Adoration hath no respect to the Images (which is contrary to the Council of *Trent*;) or that Divine Worship being due to the Being Represented, it may be likewise given to the Image. And how then could the *Gnosticks* be condemned for giving Divine Worship to the Image of Christ, which *Bellarmine* confesses; and is affirmed by *Irenæus, Epiphanius,* S. *Augustine,* and *Damascen?*

(2.) *To pray to Images of Christ, or the Blessed Virgin,* may likewise be taken in two senses. (1.) To pray to them,

them, fo as to expect to be heard by the meer Images, and fo we do not charge them with it. (2.) To pray to them, fo as to expect to be rather heard by themfelves for praying to them by their Images. And if this be not fo; to what end are the Prayers made in the Confecration of Images, for thofe that fhall pray before them? To what purpofe do fo many go in long Pilgrimages to certain Images, if they do not hope to be better heard for praying there?

But he goes on; 2. *He keeps them by him indeed, to keep in his mind the memory of the things reprefented by them.* And is this all in good Truth? We will never quarrel with them, if this be true reprefenting. No, that he dares not fay.

But, 3. *He is taught to ufe them,* p 2. But how? *by cafting his Eye upon the Pictures or Images, and thence to raife his Heart to the Prototypes.* And is this all yet? No.

But, 4. He finds a double conveniency in the ufe of them. (1.) *They reprefent at one glance*; and Men may eafily make good Reflections, as *upon the fight of a Death's Head, or old Time painted with his Fore-lock, Hour-glaſs, and Syth.* And will he undertake that Images fhall be ufed in Churches for no other end? Was the Picture of old *Time* ever *Confecrated,* or placed upon the *Altar,* or elfewhere, *that it might be worſhipped?* as the *Roman* Catechifm fpeaks of their Images. (2.) *They cure Diſtractions*; *for they call back his wandring Thoughts to the Right Object.* What is this *Right Object?* the Image, or the Perfon reprefented? And that muft be either a Creature, or God himfelf. If it be a Creature, doth not this imply that it is made a *Right Object of Worſhip?* If God himfelf; how doth an Image cure our Diſtraction, in the Worſhip of an Infinite Invifible Being; when the very Image is moft apt to diftract our Thoughts, by drawing them down from his Divine and Adorable Perfections, to the grofs and mean Reprefentations of an Image? But are we yet come to the utmoft ufe of them? No.

But, 5. *He cannot but love, honour, and refpect the Images themſelves, for the fake of thofe they reprefent.* Will this content them, and will he promife to go no further? It is hard to part upon Terms of *meer Reſpect and Decent Regard,* where there is no encroachment upon *Divine Worſhip.* And here we are at a ftand. But

But he goes further. 6. *And so he is come at last, to Veneration before Images.* And is this all? Dares he deny *Veneration to Images,* when the Council of *Trent* hath determined it? *Eisq; venerationem impartiendam?* What, is this Veneration *before Images* only? *Bellarmine* hath a Chapter on purpose to prove, that *true and proper Worship is to be given to Images.* And was he a *Misrepresenter? Suarez* saith, *It is an Article of Faith, that Worship is to be given to them.* But if the Veneration be only before them, why are they Consecrated, and set up in Places proper for Adoration?

But, 7. *To satisfy any one that he is far from making Gods of his Images, he is ready to break them into a thousand pieces.* What, a Consecrated Image? Dares he take a Crucifix from the Altar and tear it in pieces? This doth not look like *the Love, Honour, and Respect* he mentioned before, not to name *Veneration.* And I am afraid this is a strain beyond true Representing: Yet at length he hath found some pretty Parallels for the *Veneration of Images* themselves; and so we are come at last to the main Point. But this is not directly owned; yet in the way of his Representing, it is fairly insinuated by his Parallels.

1. *A Christian loves and honours his Neighbour, because he bears the Image of God in his Soul.* But doth he therefore take him and set him before him when he kneels at his Devotion, to raise his Mind, and cure his Distractions? Would he set him upon the Altar, and burn Incense before him, because of the Image of God in him? Is there no difference between the *Object of Christian Love,* and of *Divine Worship?* Nor between a Spiritual Invisible Divine Image in the Souls of Men, and a Material and Corporeal Representation?

2. *We may kiss and esteem the Bible, because it contains and represents to Us God's Word.* But when we kiss and esteem the Bible, we remember the second Commandment is in it; and we dare not break his Law, when we pretend to honour his Word. But we think there is some difference between *Reverence* and *Respect* to the *Bible,* and *falling down* before an Image. The Circumstances of the one declare it to be meer *Respect,* and a *Religious Decency*; and if the other be not *External Adoration,* we know not what it is.

3. *A*

3. *A good Preacher is loved, because he minds Men of their Duty.* But what should we say to him that should therefore kneel down and say his Prayers, and burn Candles and Incense before him, out of a respect to his good Doctrine? Did S. *Peter*, or S. *Paul* like this, when Men would have worshipped them? A good Preacher would tell them of their Duty, as they did; and take Men off from the Worship of any Creature, animate or inanimate, and direct them to worship God alone, who made Heaven and Earth.

II. *Of Worshipping Saints.*

FOR the clear stating this Controversy, these things are to be premised.

1. We do not charge them, *that they make Gods of dead Men*, i. e. that they believe the Saints to be Independent Deities. For this our Author confesses *were a most damnable Idolatry*.

2. We do not say, that the State of the Church of *Rome*, with respect to the Worship of dead Men, is as bad as Heathenism. For we acknowledg the true Saints and Martyrs to have been, not only Good and Vertuous, but Extraordinary Persons, in great Favour with God, and highly deserving our Esteem and Reverence, as well as Imitation; whereas the Heathen Deified Men, were vile and wicked Men, and deserved not the common Esteem of Mankind, according to the Accounts themselves give of them. And we own the common Doctrine and Advantages of Christianity to be preserved in the Church of *Rome*.

3. We do not deny, that they do allow some external Acts of Worship to be so proper to God alone, that they ought to be given to none else besides him. And this they call *Latria*; and we shall never dispute with them about the proper signification of a Word, when the Sense is agreed, unless they draw Inferences from it, which ought not to be allowed. To this *Latria*, they refer not only Sacrifice, but

all

all that relates to it, as Temples, Altars, and Priests: so that by their own Confession, to make these immediately and properly to the Honour of any Saint, is to make a God of that Saint, and to commit Idolatry.

4. They confess, that to pray to Saints to bestow Spiritual or Temporal Gifts upon us, were to give to them the Worship proper to God, who is the only giver of all good Things. For else I do not understand, why they should take so much pains to let us know, that whatever the Forms of their Prayers and Hymns are, yet the Intention and Spirit of the Church, is only to desire them to pray for us, and to obtain things for us by their Intercession with God.

But two things cannot be denied by them.

Sect. 25.

1. That they do use solemn Invocation of Saints in Places of Divine Worship, at the same time they make their Addresses to God himself, with all the Circumstances of External Adoration, with bended Knees, and Eyes lifted up to Heaven; and that this Practice is according to the Council of *Trent*, which not only decrees an humble Invocation of them, but declares it to be impiety to condemn mental and vocal Supplication to the Saints in Heaven.

2. That they do own making the Saints in Heaven to be their Mediators of Intercession, but not of Redemption; although Christ be our Mediator in both senses.

And upon these two Points this Controversy depends.

Let us now see what our *Representer* saith to them.

Pag. 4.

1. *His Church teaches him indeed, and he believes that it is good and profitable, to desire the Intercession of the Saints reigning with Christ in Heaven; but that they are either Gods, or his Redeemers, he is no where taught, but detests all such Doctrine.*

There are two ways of *desiring the Intercession of others for us.*

1. By way of *Friendly Request*, as an Act of mutual Charity; and so, no doubt, we may desire others here on Earth to pray for us. 2. By

2. By way of *Humble Supplication*, with all the external Acts of Adoration: and we cannot think S. *Peter*, or S. *Paul*, who refused any thing like *Adoration* from Men, would have been pleased to have seen Men fall down upon their Knees before them; and in the same posture of Devotion in which they were praying to Almighty God, to put their Names into the middle of their *Litanies*, and to pray them then to pray for them.

But how are we sure that their Church teaches no more than this? I have read over and over the Council of *Trent*, and the *Roman Catechism* about it, and I can find no such limitation of their sense there, where, if any where, it ought to be found. The Council of *Trent* mentions both the *Prayers*, and *the Help and Assistance* of the Saints which they are to fly to. If this *Help* and *Assistance* be no more than their *Prayers*, why is it mentioned as distinct? Why is *their reigning together with Christ in Heaven* spoken of, but to let us understand they have a Power to *Help* and *Assist*? For what is their Reigning to their Praying for us? But I have a further Argument to prove the Council meant more, *viz.* the Council knew the common Practices and Forms of Invocation then used and allowed, and the general Opinion, that the Saints had power to Help and Assist those who prayed to them. If the Council did not approve this, why did it insert the very words upon which that Practice was grounded? They likewise very well knew the Complaints which had been made of these things; and some of their own Communion cried shame upon some of their Hymns. *Wicelius* saith, one of them, *Salve Regina*, &c. *is full of downright Impiety, and horrible Superstition, and that others are wholly inexcusable.* Lud. *Vives* had said, *He found little difference in the Peoples Opinion of their Saints in many things, from what the Heathens had of their Gods.* These things were known; and it was in their Power to have redressed them, by declaring what the Sense of the Council was, and that whatever Forms were used, no more was to be understood by them, but *praying to them to pray for them*. Besides, the Council of *Trent*, in the very same Session, took care *about reforming the Missal and Breviary*; why was no care taken to reform

Wicel. *in Elencho Abusuum.*

Vives *in Aug. de Civit. Dei. l. 8. c. 27.*

(20)

reform these *Prayers and Hymns*, which they say are not to be construed by *the Sense of the Words*, but by *the Sense of the Church?* There was time enough taken for doing it; for the *Reformed Missal* was not published till six Years after the *Council*, nor the *Breviary* till four. In all that time, the *Prayers* and *Hymns* might easily have been altered to the *Sense of the Church*, if that were truly so. But instead of that, a very late French Writer cries out *of the necessity of Reforming the Breviaries as to these things*; wherein he confesses, *Many Hymns are still remaining, wherein those things are asked of Saints, which ought to be asked of God alone; as being delivered from the Chains of our Sins, being preserved from spiritual Maladies, and Hell Fire; being inflamed with Charity, and made fit for Heaven. In good Conscience,* saith he, *is not this joining the Saints with God himself, to ask those things of them which God alone can give?* And whatever Men talk of *the Sense of the Church*, he confesses, *the very Forms, and natural Sense of the Words, do raise another Idea in Mens Minds*; which ought to be prevented.

But doth not the Roman Catechism explain this to be the Sense of the Church? I have examined that too, with all the care I could, about this Matter. And I cannot find any necessity from thence of putting this Sense upon them. I grant in one place, where it explains *the difference of the Invocation of God and Saints*, it saith, *We are to pray to God as the Giver, and to Saints that they would obtain things of God for us*; and then it adds, *the Forms differ, that to God is, Miserere Nobis,* and *Audi Nos;* that to Saints is, *Ora pro Nobis.* Very well! And is there then no other Form owned or allowed in the Church of *Rome* to Saints besides this? Hold a little, saith the *Catechism*, for *it is lawful to make use of another Form*; and that is, *we may pray to Saints too, Ut nostri misereantur.* And how doth this now differ from that to God, but only in Number? But it adds, *that the Saints are very pitiful;* then surely we are encouraged to pray to them for *help and pity.* Yes, saith the *Catechism, we may pray to them, that being moved with pity toward us, they would help us with their Favour, and Intercession with God.* But yet this doth not clear the Matter; for elsewhere the *Roman Catechism*

[margin: *Entretiens de Philalethe & Philerene.* Part 2. p. 160, 163, 165.]

[margin: *Catech. Rom.* Part 4. c. 6. n. 2, 3.]

attributes more to *Saints* than meer *Intercession*; and we may pray to them for what is in their Power: For where it undertakes to give an exact Account of the Reason of *Invocation of Saints and Angels*; it there parallels them with *Magistrates under a King*; and faith, *they are God's Ministers in governing the Church*; *Invocandi itaque sunt quod & perpetuo Deum intuentur, & Patrocinium Salutis nostræ libentissimè suscipiunt.* What is this *Patrocinium Salutis nostræ?* Is it only *Praying and Intercession with God?* That cannot be, for it instances presently in *deliverances by Angels*, and Jacob's *praying to the Angel to bless him*, and not meerly to intercede for him. But though this is spoken of *Angels*, yet from hence it infers *the Invocation of Saints* too. But what need we insist more on this, since they do own the *Ministry of Saints* as well as Angels, with respect to the Church; and do *Canonize Saints* for particular Countries, as lately S. *Rosa* for *Peru*. And where there is such a particular Protection supposed, what incongruity is it to interpret the Form of their Prayers, according to a Doctrine so received and allowed? But of this more under the next Head.

Catech. Rom.
Part 3. c. 2.
n. 4, 6.
Cum præsint nobis Sancti & rerum nostrarum curam gerant.
Bellarm. de Sanct. Beatit. l. 1. c. 20. §. deinde. Non solum ab Angelis sed etiam à spiritibus beatorum hominum Regi & Gubernari fideles vitæ testes. Id. ib. c. 18. §. nos autem.

2. *He confesses that we are all redeemed by the Blood of Christ alone, and that he is our only Mediator of Redemption; but as for Mediators of Intercession, he doth not doubt but it is acceptable with God we should have many.*

I would ask, concerning this Distinction, the Question which *Christ* asked concerning *John*'s *Baptism*, *Is it from Heaven, or of Man?* No doubt there may be such a Distinction of *Mediators*, if God please to make them. But who hath Authority to appoint Mediators with him besides himself? Is it not usurping his Prerogative, to appoint the great Officers of his Kingdom for him? Would any Prince upon Earth allow this, *viz.* when he hath absolutely declared his Pleasure, that his own Son should present Petitions to him, that others shall take upon them to set up Masters of Requests themselves? Can any thing be plainer in the New Testament, than that God hath appointed the *Mediator of Redemption*, to be our *Mediator of Intercession*? And that his *Intercession* is founded upon his *Redemption*. As the High Priest's

John 14. 13,
14, 15, 23, 24.
Heb. 7. 25.
& 9. 7, 24.
1 Jo. 2. 1.

Priest's going into the *Holy of Holies* to intercede for the People, was upon the *Blood of the Sacrifice of Expiation*, which he carried in with him. If there were no Revelation in this Matter, there might be some reason for it. But since the Revelation is so clear in it, this distinction looks just like the *Socinians* Distinction of a *God by Nature*, and a *God by Office*; which was framed on purpose to avoid the plain Texts of Scripture which called Christ *God*. So doth this look as if it were intended to avoid that clear Text, which saith, *There is one Mediator between God and Men, the Man Christ Jesus.* Which is presently answered with this Distinction; although there be not the least ground in that or any other Text for it.

Tim. 2. 5.

Yes, saith our Author, Moses *was such a Mediator for the Israelites*; Job *for his three Friends*; Stephen *for his Persecutors:* The Romans *were desired by* S. Paul *to be his Mediator, and the* Corinthians *and* Ephesians; *so almost every sick Person desires the Congregation to be his Mediator, that is, to be remembred in their Prayers.* P. 4, 5.

But is there no difference between Men praying for one another, and desiring others to pray for them here on Earth, and an *humble Invocation* of the *Saints in Heaven* to be our *Mediators* of *Intercession* with God there?

There is a threefold disparity in the Case.

1. Here upon Earth we converse with one another as Fellow Creatures, and there is no danger of our having an Opinion thereby, that we are able to assist one another any other way than by our Prayers. But the Case is very different as to the Saints in Heaven, who by being addressed to there by such solemn Invocation, may too easily be conceived to have the Power of bestowing such Blessings upon those who call upon them.

2. Heaven is looked on by all Mankind who direct their Devotions thither, as the particular Throne of God, where he dwells, and discovers himself after another manner than he doth upon the Earth. And we are directed to pray to our *Father in Heaven*; where he is represented as infinitely above all his Creatures: and the great Concernment of Religion

gion is, to keep up the apprehenſion of this diſtance between him and them. Now it is hardly poſſible to keep it up, if in the Publick Offices of Religion, in the ſolemneſt poſtures of Devotion, with Eyes lifted up to Heaven, they do make Addreſſes, both to God and to his Creatures.

3. Men are ſure, when they pray to others on Earth to pray for them, that they do no more than they can juſtify in point of Diſcretion, when they ſpeak or write to thoſe that can underſtand what their deſire is: But no Man on Earth can be certain that the Saints in Heaven can do it: For it is agreed they cannot do it without Revelation; and no Man can be aſſured there is a Revelation; and it is not reaſonable to expect it: for they pray to Saints to pray to God for them; and they cannot tell what they pray for, unleſs God to whom they are to pray, reveal to them what it is they muſt pray to him for. Is it not then the better, the ſafer, the wiſer way, to make our Prayers to him, who we are ſure is able to hear and help us; and hath promiſed to grant what we ask in his Son's Name? But there is no *other Name*, either *under Heaven*, or *in Heaven*, whereby we can be ſaved, or our Prayers accepted, but his alone.

But our Author ſaith, *It is no part of his Faith, how the Saints in Heaven know the Prayers and Neceſſities of ſuch who addreſs themſelves to them.* P. 5.

But how comes it to be any part of his Faith, that they know them? *However he doth not doubt but God can never want means of letting the Saints know them.* P. 6. And is this a ſufficient Ground for ſolemn Invocation of Saints? God doth not want Means to let the Emperor of *Japan* know a Requeſt any one here hath to make to him; but is this a reaſonable Ground, for him at this diſtance to make it to him? God doth not want Means to let the Pope know what a mighty Service it would be to the Chriſtian World, to make a wiſe and truly Chriſtian-Reformation in the Church; but would this be a ground ſufficient for me at this Diſtance, to make a Speech to him about it? I knew a Man who underſtood not a word of Latin, but yet would needs go to hear a Latin Sermon: ſome asked him afterwards, what he meant by it? and the chief Reaſon he gave was much like this,

this, *God did not want Means to let him know what the Preacher meant.*

But after all, Suppose *God should make known to the Saints what is desired of them*; I ask, Whether this be sufficient Ground for solemn Invocation? When *Socinus* was not able to defend the *Invocation of Christ himself*, supposing that he could know our Hearts only by Revelation: And he had nothing material to say, but only that there was a Command for it; which can never be so much as pretended in this Case.

As to what he alleadges of *the Elders falling down before the Lamb, having Vials full of Odours, which are the Prayers of the Saints,* Apoc. 5. 8. It must be strained hard to be brought to this purpose, when both Ancient and Modern Interpreters take it for a Representation of what was done upon Earth, and not in Heaven. And if it were in Heaven, Prophetical Visions were never intended for a Measure of our Duties. *If the Angels do pray for Mankind,* Zech. 1. 12. Doth it therefore follow we must pray to them? But we say as the Angel did to S. *John,* Revel. 19. 10. in a like Case; *See thou do it not: worship God.*

III. *Of Addressing more Supplications to the* Virgin Mary, *than to Christ.*

HEre is no need of farther stating the Question; this only relating to the extraordinary Service of the blessed Virgin. And therefore we are presently to attend his Motions.

He believes it damnable to think the Virgin Mary *more powerful in Heaven than Christ, or that she can in any thing command him.* P. 6.

But in good earnest, Is it not damnable, unless a Man thinks the Blessed Virgin *more powerful than Christ?* Suppose one should think her to have *an equal share of Power with Christ*; Is this damnable, or not? Is it not setting up a Creature equal with God?

But

But what thinks he then of those who have attributed an universal Dominion to her, over Angels, Men, and Devils? What thinks he not only of *Psalters*, but of a *Creed*, *Litany*, and all the *Hymns* of *Scripture* being applied to her? All which was done by a Canonized Saint in their Church; and the Books printed out of the *Vatican* Manuscripts, and dedicated to the Pope. And there we find something more than an *Ora pro nobis* in the *Litany*; for there is *Parce nobis, Domina*; Spare us, good Lady: and, *Ab omni malo, libera nos, Domina*; From all Evil, Good Lady, deliver us.

S. Bonavent. *Opusc. Tom.* 1. *ad fin.*

What thinks he of another Canonized Saint, who said, these two Propositions are both true, *All things are subject to God's Command, even the Virgin*; and *all things are subject to the Command of the Virgin, even God*. Was this damnable in a Canonized Saint?

S. Bernardin. *Sen. apud Bernadin. à Bustis Marial.* Part 12. Serm. 2.

What thinks he of the noted Hymn?

O felix Puerpera nostra pians scelera
Jure Matris impera Redemptori!

Was not this damnable? And I have not only seen it in the old *Paris Missal*, but *Balinghem* a Jesuit, saith, it was in the Missals of *Tournay, Liege, Amiens, Artois*, and the old *Roman*. I could produce many other Passages cited by him out of the old *Offices* to the same purpose; but I forbear.

Balinghem. *Parnass. Marian.* p. 268.

But I cannot omit the Approbation given to the blasphemous saying of S. *Bernardin* by *Mendoza*, (who endeavours to prove *the blessed Virgin's Kingdom, not to be a Metaphorical, but a true and real Kingdom*). And by *Salazar*, another noted Jesuit, who saith, *Her Kingdom is as large as her Son's*. And we have lately seen how far this Divinity is spread, for not many Years since, this Proposition was sent from *Mexico*,

Mendoza. *Virid. Sacr.* l. 2, *Probl.* 1. & 4. Salazar pro Immac. Concept. c. 32.

Filius non tantum tenetur audire Matrem, sed & obedire;

The Son is bound not only to hear, but to obey his Mother. And is it still damnable for to say, *she commands him*?

Hier. Peres de Nueros Lapidicina Sacra Tr. 1. Sect. 12. N. 148.

Pag. 7.

Vvidav. Ser.
l. 2. Probl. 2.
N. 11.

But our Author saith, What-ever esteem they have for her, *They own her still as a Creature.* Is he sure of that? What thinks he of another Saying, which *Mendoza* approves of, viz. of Christ's saying to his Mother, *As thou hast communicated Humanity to me, I will communicate my Deity to thee.*

But it may be said, *We are by no means to judg the sense of a Church by some Mens extravagant sayings.*

I grant it. But I have something considerable to reply; viz. That we may easily judg which way the Guides of that Church incline, by this following passage: About ten Years since a Gentleman of that Communion published a Book, called, *Wholsome Advice to the Worshippers of the blessed Virgin*; and the whole design of it, being printed in Latin and French, was to bring the People of that Church to a bare *Ora pro nobis* to the *blessed Virgin.* But this was so far from being approved, that the Book was condemned at *Rome*, and vehemently opposed by the Jesuits in *France*; and a whole Volume published against it.

La voitable
Devotion avers
la S. Vierge E-
table & Defen-
du par le Pere
Crasset à Paris,
A. D. 1679.

Here I have reason to enquire, Whether the Virgin *Mary* then, according to the sense of the Church of *Rome*, be only a *Mediatrix* of *Intercession* or not, since so large Power and Dominion is attributed to her? And why should not her Suppliants go beyond an *Ora pro nobis*, if this Doctrine be received; as it must be, if the contrary cannot be endured? For that Author allowed her *Intercession*, and *Prayer to her* on that account; but he found fault with those who said, *she had a Kingdom divided with her Son*; that *she was the Mother of Mercy, or was a Co-Saviour, or Co-Redemptrix*; or that *she was to be worshipped with* Latria; or that *Men were to be Slaves to her.* Now, if these things must not be touched without Censure, and no Censure pass on the other Books; is it not easy to judg, which is more agreeable to the Spirit of the Guides of that Church?

Monita Salu-
taria B. V.
Mariæ ad Cul-
tores suos indis-
cretos §. 3. n.
55. §. 4.

Contemplations of the Life and Glory of Holy *Mary*, the Mother of Jesus, *A.D. 1685.*

But we have a fresh Instance of this kind at home, in a Book very lately published; *Permissu Superiorum.* There we are told in the Epistle, That not only *the blessed Virgin is the Empress of Seraphims——the most exact Original of Practical Perfection which the Omnipotency of God ever drew; but that*

that by innumerable Titles she claims the utmost Duty of every Christian, as a proper Homage to her Greatness. What can be said more of the Son of God in our Nature? In the Book it self she is said to be *Queen of Angels, Patroness of the Church, Advocate of Sinners; that the Power of* Mary *in the Kingdom of Jesus, is suitable to her Maternity, and other Priviledges of Grace; and therefore by it she justly claims a Servitude from all pure Creatures.* But wherein doth this *special Devotion* to her consist? He names several Particulars. {Pag. 4.} {Pag. 8.}

1. *In having an inward, cordial and passionate value of the Maternity of* Mary, *and all other Excellencies proper to, and inseparable from the Mother of God.*

2. *In External Acts of Worship, of eminent Servitude towards her, by reason of the Amplitude of her Power in the Empire of Jesus.* And can we imagine these should go no farther, than a poor *Ora pro nobis?* He instances in these External Acts of her Worship. (1.) *Frequent visiting holy Places dedicated to her Honour.* And are not those her Temples then? which *Bellarmine* confesses to be a peculiar part of the Worship due to God. And the Distinction of *Basilicæ* cannot hold here: because he believes the Assumption of the Blessed Virgin; and he will not pretend *to her Honour* is only for Discrimination. (2.) *A special Reverence towards Images representing her Person.* (3.) *Performing some daily Devotions containing her Praises, congratulating her Excellency, or imploring her Mediation; and by oft calling upon the Sacred Name of* holy Mary, *&c.* {Bellarmin. *de Cultu Sanct. l.* 3. *c.* 4. *inif.*}

(3.) *In having a firm and unshaken Confidence in her Patronage amidst the greatest of our inward Conflicts, and outward Tribulations; through a strong Judgment of her eminent Power within the Empire of Jesus, grounded upon the singular Prerogative of her Divine Maternity.* I have not Patience to transcribe more, but refer the Reader to the Book it self; only the eighth Particular of *special Devotion* is so remarkable, that it ought not to be passed over, viz. *Entring a solemn Covenant with Holy* Mary, *to be for ever her Servant, Client and Devote under some special Rule, Society or Form of Life, and thereby dedicating our Persons, Concerns, Actions, and all the Moments and Events of our Life to Jesus, under the Protection* {Pag. 12.}

tection *of his Divine Mother, chusing her to be our Adoptive Mother, Patroness and Advocate; and intrusting her with what we are, have, do or hope, in Life, Death, and through all Eternity.* And is all this no more than an *Ora pro nobis?* And

Pag. 14. it follows, *Put your self wholly under her Protection.* What a pitiful thing was the old *Collyridian* Cake, in comparison of these special Acts of Devotion to her! But there are some extraordinary strains of Devotion afterwards, which it is pity to pass over. As, *I will ever observe thee as my*

Pag. 22. *Soveraign Lady, Adoptive Mother, and most powerful Patroness; relying on thy Bowels of Mercy, in all my Wants, Petitions, and Tribulations of Body and Mind.* Could any thing greater be said to the Eternal Son of God? And in the *Praise:*

Verf. Open my Lips, O Mother of Jesus.
Resp. And my Soul shall speak forth thy Praise.
Verf. Divine Lady, be intent to my Aid.
Resp. Graciously make haste to help me.
Verf. Glory be to Jesus and Mary.
Resp. As it was, is, and ever shall be.

Then follows the Eighth *Psalm*, applied thus to her.

Pag. 24. Mary, *Mother of Jesus, how wonderful is thy Name, even unto the Ends of the Earth!*
All Magnificence be given to Mary, *and let her be exalted above the Stars and Angels.*
Reign on high as Queen of Seraphims and Saints; and be thou crowned with Honour, and Glory, &c.
Glory be to Jesus and Mary, *&c.*

In the next Page, follows a *Cantique* in imitation of the *Te Deum*.

Pag. 25. *Let us praise thee, O Mother of Jesus? Let us acknowledg thee our Soveraign Lady.*
Let Men and Angels give Honour to thee, the first conceived of all pure Creatures, &c.

I think I need mention no more; only three things I shall observe, (1.) That this is now printed *Permissu Superiorum*; and we thank them for the seasonableness of it, in helping us in *true Representing*, what their allowed Doctrines and Practices are. (2.) That this is published in English, that our People, as well as theirs, may be convinced how far we have been from unjust charging them as to such things as these. (3.) That at the same time they plead for keeping the Bible out of the hands of the People; wherein their Discretion is so far to be commended, since the Scripture, and this new Scheme of Devotion, can never stand together. There being not one word in the Bible towards it, but very much against it; and the Psalms and Hymns must be *burlesqu'd* to sound that way.

But what saith our Author to their *Rosaries*, wherein there are *ten Ave Maries to one Pater noster*; which is accounted a special piece of Devotion; and great things are said of the Effects of it by *Alanus de Rupe*, and many others?

1. As to the *Ave Maries*, he saith, *there is no more Dishonour to God in reciting the Angelical Salutation, than in the first pronouncing it by the Angel* Gabriel *and* Elizabeth. But it may not be altogether so pertinent. But doth he really think they said the whole *Ave Maria*, as it is used among them? Did the Angel and *Elizabeth* say, *Sancta Maria, Mater Dei, ora pro nobis peccatoribus, nunc & in hora mortis nostræ*? If not, to what purpose are they mentioned here? [Pag. 7.]

2. As to the *Repetition*; that, he saith, *is no more an idle Superstition, than* David's *repeating the same words 26 times in the 136 Psalm.* But what is this to the Question, *why more Supplications to the blessed Virgin, than to Christ?* And not one word of Answer is given to it. But *Alanus de Rupe* answers it roundly, *Because the blessed Virgin is our Mediatrix to Christ, the Mother of Mercy, and the special Patroness of Sinners.* This is indeed true representing. [Alanus de Rupe de usu Psalterii, l. 1. c. 5.]

E   IV. Of

IV. *Of paying Divine Worship to Reliques.*

FOR the right understanding this Controversy, we are to consider,

1. That there is a due Veneration to the Bodies of Saints and Martyrs, allowed on both sides; and there is an undue Worship of them, which is disowned on both sides. The due Veneration is, a Religious Decency to be observed towards them; which lies in avoiding any thing like Contempt or Dishonour to them, and using all such Testimonies of Respect and Decency, which becomes the Remains of Excellent Persons; provided we are satisfied of their Sincerity, without having recourse to Divine Omnipotency to prove them: which *Ferrandus* the Jesuit runs so much to, to prove the Truth of many Reliques, worshipped in the Church of *Rome* in many places at once. But that it is possible to exceed in the Worship of true Reliques, even *Bellarmin* confesseth, who says, *that God took away the Body of* Moses, *lest the People should give Divine Worship to it.* And St. *Jerom*, as hot as he was against *Vigilantius*, yet he utterly denied giving any Adoration to the Reliques of Martyrs. It seems then it is very possible to exceed that way.

Ferrandi. Disquisitio Reliquiaria.

De Imag. Sanct. l. 2. c. 4.

2. The Question then is, Whether those Acts of Worship which are allowed in the Church of *Rome*, do not go beyond due Veneration? For it is unreasonable to suppose those who give it, to believe those Reliques to be Gods; and therefore it must be such a Worship as is given to them, supposing them to be only Reliques of such Persons. The Council of *Trent* decrees Honour and Veneration to be given to them, but never determines what is due, and what not: it forbids all Excesses in drinking and eating, in the visiting of Reliques; but not a word of Excesses in worshipping of them, unless it be comprehended under the name of Superstition. But *Superstition* lies in something forbidden, according to their notion of it: therefore, if there be no Prohibition

bition by the Church, there can be no Superstition in the Worship of them. And if they had thought there had been any in the known Practices of the Church, they would certainly have mentioned them; and because they did not, we ought in Reason to look on them as allowed. And yet not only *Cassander* complains of the great Superstition about them; but even the *Wallenbergii* lately confess, that the Abuses therein, have not only been offensive to us, but to themselves too.

Cassand. Consul.
Art. 21. *Tract.*
special 4. *Controv.* 4.

But what saith our *Representer* to them?

He believes it damnable to think there's any Divinity in the Reliques of Saints, or to adore them with Divine Honour. P. 7. But what is this adoring them with Divine Honour? A true Representer ought to have told us what he meant by it, when the whole Controversy depends upon it. Is it only saying Mass to Reliques, or believing them to be Gods? Is there no giving Divine Honour by Prostration, burning of Incense, &c. Nothing in expecting help from them? Yes, *If it be from any hidden Power of their own.* But here is a very hard Question: If a Man doth not believe it to be an intrinsick Power in the Reliques, may a Man safely go to them, *Opis impetrandæ causâ*, as the Council of *Trent* saith, in hopes of Relief from them? Is it not possible for the Devil to appear with *Samuel*'s true Body, and make use of the Relique of a Saint to a very bad end? Then, say I, no Reliques can secure Men against the Imposture of Evil Spirits, who, by God's Permission, may do strange things with the very Reliques of Saints.

But God hath visibly worked by them, saith our Author, *by making them Instruments of many Miracles; and it is as easie for him to do it now.* P. 8, 9. This is the force of all he saith. To which I answer,

1. It is a very bold thing to call in God's Omnipotency, where God himself hath never declared he will use his Power; for it is under his own Command, and not ours. But there is no Reason to deduce the Consequence of using it now, because he hath done it formerly. And that they may not think this is cavilling in us, I desire them to read *Pere Annat*'s Answer to the Jansenists pretended Miracle at *Port*

Rabat. Joy de Jesuit, A. D. 1656.

Port Royal, viz. of the Cure wrought by one of our Saviour's Thorns. There he gives another account of such Miracles than would be taken from us. But where he saith, *It is as much for the Honour of God's Name to work such Miracles now*; their own Authors will tell him the contrary; and that there is no such Reason now, as in former times, when Religion was to be confirmed by them; and when Martyrs suffered upon the sole account of the Truth of it; and therefore their Reputation had a great Influence upon converting the unbelieving World.

2. Suppose it be granted, yet it proves not any Religious Worship to be given to them. For I shall seriously ask an important Question: Whether they do really believe, any greater Miracles have ever been done by Reliques, than were done by the Brazen Serpent? And yet, although that was set up by God's own Appointment, when it began to be worshipped after an undue manner; it was thought fit by *Hezekiah* to be broken in pieces. What now was the undue Worship they gave to it? Did they believe the Serpent, which could neither move nor understand, was it self a God? *But they did burn Incense to it*. And did that make a God of it? Suppose Men burn Incense to Reliques; what then, are they made Gods presently? Suppose they do not, but place them upon Altars, carry them in Procession, fall down before them, with intention to shew the Honour they do them; are not these as much as burning a little Incense, which could not signify so much Honour as the other do? and it is hard then to make the one unlawful, and not the other.

V. *Of the Eucharist.*

THere are two material Points under this Head which are to be examined, because he endeavours to set them off with all the advantage he can, *viz.* Adoration of the Host, and Transubstantiation.

I. *Of the Adoration of the Host.*

1. The Question is far enough from being, Whether it be lawful to commit Idolatry? as our *Representer* puts it. For the *Misrepresenter* saith, *That a Papist believes it lawful to commit Idolatry:* and to clear this, our Author gravely saith, *He believes it unlawful to commit Idolatry*, pag. 9. As though any Men ever owned it to be lawful: Which is, as if the Question were, Whether such a Man committed Adultery, and he should think to clear himself by saying, he believed it unlawful to commit Adultery.

2. The Question is not, Whether Christ may be lawfully adored by us in the Celebration of the Eucharist; which we are so far from denying, that our Church requires our receiving it in the posture of Adoration.

3. The true Question is, Whether the Body of Christ, being supposed to be present in the Host by Transubstantiation, be a sufficient Ground to give the same Adoration to the Host, which they would do to the Person of Christ?

And that this is the true state of the Question, will appear by these things.

1. The Council of *Trent* first defined Transubstantiation, and from thence inferred *Adoration of the Host*; as is most evident to any one that will read the fourth and fifth Decrees of the Thirteenth Session: *Nullus itaque dubitandi locus*, &c. *i. e.* If Transubstantiation be true, then Adoration follows. It's true, the sixth Canon only speaks of *Christ being there worshipped*; but that ought to be compared with the first, second, and fourth Canons, where the Doctrine of *Transubstantiation* is fully set down, as the Foundation of that *Adoration*.

2. The *Adoration* is not fixed on the *Person of Christ*, as *separate from the Host*, but as making *one Object* of Worship together with it. And so the Council of *Trent* declares in the sixth Decree; when it saith, *The Sacrament is never the less to be adored, because it was instituted to be received*. This cannot be otherwise understood, than as relating to the Sacrament: and so *that* what ever it be, must be granted to

be the Object of Adoration. 'By the Sacrament, saith Cardinal *Pallavicini*, is understood the Object made up of the Body of Christ, and the Accidents.' The Worship then being confessed to be Adoration, which is due to God alone, and that Adoration directed to the Sacrament as its proper Object; the Question now is, Whether such a Supposition in the Sacrament, doth justify that Adoration?

<small>Pallavicin. Hist. Concil. Trident. l. 12. c. 6.</small>

Our Author saith, *He accounteth it most damnable to worship or adore any breaden God, or to give Divine Honour to any Elements of Bread and Wine.* p. 9.

Then, I say, by his own confession, if it be only Bread, he commits Idolatry; for the Adoration he cannot deny. But our *Representer* loves ambiguous Expressions, which to the People sound very well, but have no sincere meaning: for what is it he understands by his *breaden God?* If it be that he worships a God which himself supposes to be nothing but Bread, we do not charge him with it; but if it be what we beleive it to be, the Substance of Bread, but himself believes to be turned into the Body of Christ, then he cannot deny his Adoration to be given to it.

All that can excuse them is, the Supposition; and whether that will or not, is now to be consider'd.

1. If it be not true, themselves grant it to be Idolatry. The Testimonies of Bishop *Fisher*, and *Costerus*, are so well known to this purpose, that I shall not repeat them. And *Catharinus*, a Divine of Note in the Council of *Trent*, confesses it is Idolatry to worship an unconsecrated Host, although the Person, through a Mistake, believes it Consecrated. And he quotes St. *Thomas* and *Paludanus* for his Opinion; and gives this Reason for it; *because Christ is not worshipped simply in the Sacrament, but as he is under the Species; and therefore if he be not so present, a Creature hath Divine Worship given it. As those were guilty of Idolatry, who worshipped any Creatures of old, supposing God to be there, as that he was the Soul of the World. They were not excused,* saith he, *that they thought they worshipped but one God; because they worshipped him as present in such a manner, as he was not.* And this Book of his, he saith, in the Review of it, *was seen and approved by the Pope's Order, by their Divines at Paris.*

<small>Roffins. c. Oecolamp. l. 1. c. 2. Coster. Euchirid. c. 8. n. 10.</small>

<small>Catharin. in Cajet. p. 133, &c. Ed. Paris. 1535</small>

<small>Lugdun. 1542.</small>

2. If

2. *If the Bread were taken to be God,* our Author doth not deny it would be Idolatry, for that were to worſhip a breaden God. Yet here would be a Miſtake, and a groſs one; yet this Miſtake would not excuſe the Perſons committing it from moſt damnable Idolatry, as he confeſſes: Why then ſhould the other Miſtake excuſe them, when they ſuppoſe the Subſtance of the Bread not to be there, but the Body of Chriſt to be under the Species? *Yes,* ſay they, *then no Creature is ſuppoſed to be the Object of Worſhip.* But when the Bread is ſuppoſed to be God, it muſt be ſuppoſed not to be a Creature. There is no Anſwer to be given in this Caſe, *but that the Bread really is a Creature, whatſoever they imagined*; and if this Miſtake did not excuſe, neither can the other.

II. *Of Tranſubſtantiation.*

Three Things our Author goes upon, with reſpect to this.

1. He ſuppoſes Chriſt's words to be clear for it.
2. He ſhews the poſſibility of it, from God's Omnipotency. P.9,10,11,12.
3. He argues againſt the Teſtimony or Evidence of Senſe or Reaſon in this Caſe, from ſome parallel Inſtances, as he thinks.

1. *He believes Jeſus Chriſt made his Words good, pronounced at his laſt Supper, really giving his Body and Blood to his Apoſtles; the Subſtance of Bread and Wine being, by his powerful Words, changed into his own Body and Blood; the Species only, or Accidents of the Bread and Wine, remaining as before. The ſame he believes of the Euchariſt conſecrated now by Prieſts.*

This is a very eaſy way, of taking it for granted that the words are clear for Tranſubſtantiation. And from no better Ground, to fly to God's Omnipotency to make it good, is as if one ſhould ſuppoſe Chriſt really to be turned into a Rock, a Vine, a Door; becauſe the words are every jot as clear, and then call in God's Omnipotency, which is as effectual to make them good. I confeſs, theſe words are ſo far from being clear to me for Tranſubſtantiation, that if I had

had never heard of it, I should never have thought of it, from these or any other words of Scripture, *i. e.* not barely considering the sound of words, but the Eastern Idioms of speaking; the Circumstances of our Saviour's real Body at that time when he spake them; the uncouth way of feeding on Christ's real Body, without any Objection made against it by his Disciples; the Key our Saviour elsewhere gives for understanding the manner of eating his Flesh; and withal, if these words be literally and strictly understood, they must make the Substance of Bread to be Christ's Body; for that is unavoidably the literal sense of the words. For can any Men take *This* to be any thing but this Bread, who attend to the common sense and meaning of Words, and the strict Rules of Interpretation? Yet this sense will by no means be allow'd; for then all that can be inferr'd from these words is, that when Christ spake these words, *The Bread was his Body*. But either Christ meant the *Bread* by *This*, or he did not; if he did, the former Proposition is unavoidable in the literal Sense; if he did not, then by virtue of these words, the Bread could ne'er be turned into the Body of Christ. For that only could be made the Body of Christ which was meant, when Christ said, *This is my Body*. This seems to me to be as plain and convincing as any Demonstration in *Euclid*. Which hath often made me wonder at those who talk so confidently of the plain Letter of Scripture, being for this Doctrine of Transubstantiation. But several Divines of the Church of *Rome*, understood themselves better, and have confessed, That this Doctrine could not be drawn out of the literal sense of these words; as it were easy to shew, if it had not been lately done already. It is enough here to observe, that *Vasquez* confesseth it of *Scotus, Durandus, Palndanus, Ockam, Cameracensis*; and himself yields that they do not, and cannot signify expresly the Change of the Bread and Wine into the Body of Christ. For how can, *This is my Body*, literally signify, this is changed into my Body? If that Proposition were literally true, *This is my Body*, it overthrows the change; For how can a thing be changed into that which it is already?

Vasq. in 3 Part. Disc. 180. Q. 75. Art. 2. C. 5.

2. *He believes Christ being equal to his Father in Truth and Omnipotency, can make his Words good.* We do not in the least
dispute

dispute Christ's Omnipotency, but we may their familiar way of making use of it to help them out, when Sense and Reason fail them. And therefore *Cajetan* well said; 'We 'ought not to dispute about God's Absolute Power in the 'Doctrine of the Sacraments, being things of such constant 'use; and that it is a foolish thing to attribute to the Sacra-'ment all that God can do.

Cajetan. in 3 Part. Q. 75. Art. 1, 2, 3.

But we must consider what he saith against *Sense and Reason*. For the believing this *Mystery*, he does not at all think it meet for any *Christian* to appeal from *Christ's Words*, to his own *Senses or Reason*, for the examining the Truth of what he hath said, but rather to submit his Senses and Reason to Christ's Words in the obsequiousness of Faith. What! whether we know this to be the meaning of Christ's Words, or not? And thus we shall be bound to submit to every absurd Interpretation of Scripture, because we must not use our Senses or Reason for examining the Truth of what is said there. Can any thing be plainer said in Scripture, than that God hath Eyes, and Ears, and Hands? Must now every Man yield to this *in the obsequiousness of Faith*, without examining it by Principles of Common Reason? And we think we are therefore bound to put another Sense upon those Expressions, because they imply a Repugnancy to the Divine Perfections. Why not then where something is implied which is repugnant to the Nature of Christ's Body, as well as to our Senses? But the Question about judging in this Matter by our Senses, is not, as our Author is willing to suppose, *viz.* Whether our Senses are to be believed, against a clear and express Divine Revelation; but whether the Judgment of our Senses and Reason is not to be made use of for finding out the true sense of this Revelation? And we think there is great reason for it.

(1.) Because we have no more certain way of judging the Substance of a Body, than by our Senses. We do not say our Senses go beyond the Accidents; but we say, our Senses, by those Accidents, do assure us of the bodily Substance, or else it were impossible for us to know there is any such thing in the World.

(2.) Because Christ did himself appeal to the Judgment of his Disciples Senses concerning the Truth of his own

S. Luk. 24. 39. Body after the Resurrection ; *Behold my Hands and my Feet, that it is I my self: handle and see, for a Spirit hath not Flesh and Bones, as ye see me have.* Now we think we have reason to allow the same *Criterion* which Christ himself did about the very same Body. Unless he had then told his Disciples, that there was to be *another supernatural manner of Existence* of the same Body, concerning which their Senses were not to be Judges.

(3.) Some of the most important Articles of the Christian Faith do suppose the Judgment of our Senses to be true. As about the Truth of Christ's Body; whether he had really a Body, or only the outward Accidents and Appearance of a Body? if he had not, he did not really suffer upon the Cross, and so the Sacrifice of Propitiation there offered up to the Father for the Sins of Mankind, is lost. There was a great Controversy in St. *John*'s time, and afterwards, Whether Christ had any real Body? Those who denied it, brought Revelation for it; those who asserted it, proved it by their Senses, as S. *John* himself, *That which we have seen, and heard, and our hands have handled,* &c. He doth not tell Men, they must submit their Sense and Reason to the pretence of Revelation; but they ought to adhere to the Judgment of their Senses concerning the Reality of Christ's Body. Since therefore Christ himself appealed to it, the Apostles made use of it, without any Caution or Limitation, we have great reason to rely still on the Judgment of our Senses concerning the same Object, *viz.* the Body of Christ.

1 S. Joh. 1. 1, 3.

3. But we must now consider his Instances to overthrow the Judgment of our Senses and Reason in this Point.

1. *He believes Christ to be God, though to Senses he seemed nothing but Man.* Do we ever pretend to judg of Christ's Divinity by our Senses? How then can this be pertinent, when our only Dispute is about judging his Body, and the Substance of Bread and Wine by them? And yet the Senses were of great use as to the proof of his Divinity by the Miracles which he wrought ? which if they had been like the pretended Miracles in Transubstantiation, could have convinced no Man, because they could never see them.

2. *He believes the Holy Ghost descended on our Saviour, tho Senses or Reason could discover it to be nothing but a Dove.* If there

there were no reason to judg otherwise, the Judgment of Sense were to be followed: but since the Scripture declares it was the Holy Ghost descending as a Dove, we have no reason to question that Revelation. For we do not pretend that our Senses are so far Judges of Divine Appearances, as to exclude the possibility of God's assuming the shape and figure of his Creature when he pleases, by moulding the substance of a real Body into such a Representation. Thus we do not deny the possibility of an appearance of the Holy Ghost under Bread and Wine, if God thought fit, any more than under a Dove; and in this Case we do not pretend that our Senses can exclude the presence of a Spirit under the Elements; but that is very different from the present Case, for here the Substance is supposed to be gone, and nothing but Accidents remaining; and no spiritual Presence of Christ is denied, but that of his Body, the very same Body which suffered on the Cross.

3. *He believes the Man who appeared to* Joshua, *(ch.* 5. 13.) *and the three Men to* Abraham, *(Gen.* 18.) *were really and substantially no Men, notwithstanding all the Information and Evidence of Sense to the contrary, from their Colour, Features, Proportion, Talking, Eating, and many others.* And what follows from hence, but that Spiritual Invisible Substances may be under the appearance of Bodies, and that our Senses cannot be Judges of them? Which is not our Question, but, Whether Bodies can be so present after the manner of Spirits, as to lose all the natural Properties of Bodies? and whether a Material Substance can be lost, under all the Accidents proper to it, so as our Senses cannot be proper Judges of one by the other?

But our Author seems to grant this, in a natural way of the Existence of a Body: but he saith, *Christ gives to his Body a supernatural manner of Existence, by which being left without extension of Parts, and rendred independent of Place, it may be one and the same in many Places at once, and whole in every part of the Symbols, and not obnoxious to any corporeal contingencies.*

This is to me a Mystery beyond all comprehension by Sense or Reason; and there is certainly a great difference between governing our Understandings, and giving them up, as we must do if this Doctrine hold good; for it overthrows any fixed

fixed Principles of Reason in Mankind concerning the Nature and Properties of Bodies.

For, 1. We must still suppose the Body of Christ to be the very same individual Body which suffered upon the Cross; but if it had no extension of Parts, and be reckoned independent upon Place, it ceaseth to be a Body. It is granted, that after a natural way of Existence, a Body cannot be in more Places than one : but let the way of Existence be what it will, if it be a Body, it must be finite ; if finite, it must be limited and circumscribed ; if it be circumscribed within one place, it cannot be in more places, for that is to make it circumscribed, and not circumscribed ; undivided from it self, and divided from it self at the same time. Which is a manifest Contradiction, which doth not depend only on Quantity or Extension, but upon the essential Unity of a Body.

2. If it be possible for a Body to be in several places by *a supernatural Existence*; why may not the same Body be in several Places by *a Natural Existence?* Is it not because Extension and Circumscription are so necessary to it, that in a natural Way it can be but in one Place ? Then it follows that these are essential Properties of Bodies ; so that no true Body can be conceived without them.

3. This *Supernatural Existence* doth not hinder the Body's being individually present in one Place : My meaning is this ; A Priest Consecrates an Host at *London*, and another at *York*: is the Body of Christ at *London*, so present there by virtue of Consecration, as to be present at *York* too, by this *Supernatural Existence?* What then doth the Consecration at *York* produce ? If it be not, then its Presence is limited to the Host, where the Consecration is made ; and if it be so limited, then this *Supernatural Existence* cannot take off its Relation to Place.

4. The same Body would be liable to the greatest Contradictions imaginable : For the same Body after this *supernatural way of Existence*, may not only be above and below, within and without, near and far off from it self : but it may be hot and cold, dead and alive ; yea, in Heaven and Hell at once.

5. What is it that makes it still a Body after this *supernatural way of Existence*, &c. if it lose extension and dependency

dency on place? If it be only an aptitude to extenſion, when that *ſupernatural Exiſtence* is taken off, then it muſt either be without quantity, or with it. If it be without quantity, how can it be a Body? if with quantity, how is it poſſible to be without Extenſion?

6. This confounds all the differences of Greater and Leſs, as well as of Diſtance and Nearneſs. For upon this Suppoſition, a thing really greater may be contained within a leſs: for the whole Organical Body of Chriſt, with all its Parts, may be brought within the compaſs of a Wafer; and the whole be in every part without any diſtance between Head and Feet.

7. This makes Chriſt to have but one Body, and yet to have as many Bodies as there are conſecrated Hoſts. No, ſaith our Author, *This ſupernatural manner of Exiſtence is without danger of multiplying his Body, or making as many Chriſts as Altars.* P. 11. But how this can be, is paſt all human Underſtanding: For every Conſecration hath its Effect, which is ſuppoſed to be the Converſion of the Subſtance of the Bread into the Body of Chriſt. Now, when a Prieſt at *London* converts the Bread into the Body of Chriſt there, he doth it not into the Body of Chriſt at *York*, but the Prieſt there doth it; therefore the Body of Chriſt at *London*, is different from that at *York*; or elſe the Converſion at *London* would be into the Body, as at *York*. But if not, what is the ſubſtantial Term of this ſubſtantial Change, where nothing but an accidental Mode doth follow? If there be any ſuch Term, whether that muſt not be a Production of ſomething which was not before; and if it be ſo, Chriſt muſt have as many new Bodies, as there are Conſecrations.

8. This makes that which hath no particular Subſiſtence of its own, to be the Subject of a ſubſtantial Change; for this is the condition of Chriſt's Body, whatever its manner of Exiſtence be, after the Hypoſtatical Union to the Divine Nature. For, when *Bellarmin*, *Petavius*, and others of their greateſt Divines, undertake, againſt *Neſtorius*, to explain the Hypoſtatical Union, they tell us, it conſiſts in this, that the Human Nature loſeth it proper Subſiſtence, and is aſſumed into the Subſiſtence of the Divine Nature. Bellarm. *di Incarn. l.* 3. *c.* 8. Petav. *de Incarnatione.* p. 6. *c.* 1. §. 3.

From whence I infer, That the Body of Christ, having no proper Subsistence of its own, there can be no substantial Change into that which hath no proper Subsistence, but into that which hath; and consequently the Change must be into the Divine Nature principally; from whence it will follow, the Elements losing their Subsistence, upon Consecration the Divinity must be united hypostatically to them, as to the Human Nature; and so there will be as many Hypostatical Unions, as there are Consecrations. And so this Doctrine not only confounds Sense and Reason, but the Mysteries of Christ's Incarnation too: Which I think is sufficient for this Head.

VI. Of Merits and Good Works.

FOR the true stating this Controversy, we are to observe;

1. That we do not charge those of the Church of *Rome, That they believe Christ's Death and Passion to be ineffectual and insignificant, and that they have no dependence on the Merits of his Sufferings, or the Mercy of God for attaining Salvation; but that they are to be saved only by their own Merits and Good Works*; as the Misrepresenter saith, *Pag.* 12.

2. We do not charge them with denying the *necessity of Divine Grace in order to Merit; or with asserting that they can merit independently thereupon.*

3. We do by no means dispute about the *Necessity of Good Works,* in order to the Reward of another Life; or assert that Christ's Merits will save Men without *working out their own Salvation*; but do firmly believe, that *God will judg Men according to their Works.*

The Question then is, *Whether the Goods Works of a just Man,* as our Author expresses it, *are truly meritorious of Eternal Life?* Which he affirms, but qualifies with saying, *That they proceed from Grace, and that through God's Goodness and Promise, they are truly meritorious.* But the Council of *Trent denounces an Anathema against those who deny the Good Works of justified Persons, to be truly meritorious of the increase of Grace, and of Eternal Life.*

Pag. 13.

Concil. Trident. Sess. 6. Can. 32.

Here

Here then lie the Points in difference, (1.) Whether such Good Works can be said to be *truly meritorious*? (2.) Whether those who deny it, deserve an *Anathema* for so doing? As to what relates to *God's Acceptance and Allowance, and his Goodness and Promise*, we freely own all that he saith about it; and if no more be meant, what need an *Anathema* about this matter? There must therefore be something beyond this, when Good Works are not only said to be *truly meritorious*, but we are cursed if we do not say the same.

To make any thing *truly meritorious*, we must suppose these Conditions requisite.

1. That what we pretend to merit by, be our own free Act.
2. That it be not defective.
3. That there be an Equality between it, and the Reward due to it.
4. That there be an Obligation in point of Justice, to give that Reward to him that doth it.

And from these Considerations, we deny that Good Works, even of justified Persons, can be *truly meritorious*.

1. It is granted by themselves, That what is *truly meritorious*, must be a free Act of the Person who doth it. Now the Good Works of justified Persons cannot be said to be their own free Acts, if the Power of doing them depend upon Divine Assistance, and there was an antecedent Obligation upon them to perform them: So that they can do nothing but what they are bound to, as God's Creatures; and their very Power of doing it is from the Grace of God. If Men pretended to merit at anothers hands by what God gives, there were some colour for it; but to merit from God himself by what he gives us, seems very incongruous. If I owe a Man an 100*l.* and another knowing me unable to pay it, gives me so much to pay the Debt, this is no more than what may be called strict Payment, as to the Creditor; but if the Creditor himself gives me this 100*l.* to pay himself with, will any Man call this strict Payment? He may call it so himself, if he pleases, but that only shews his Kindness

Meritum est Actio libera cui Merces debetur ex justitia. Coster. *Enchirid. de Meritis bon. Oper. c. 7.*

In quantum homo propria a-luntate facit id quod debet, mi-retur apud Deum, alioquin reddere debitum non esset merito-rium. Aquin. 1, 2. qu. 114. ar. tic. 1. resp. ad 1.

ness and Favour; but it doth not look very modestly or gratefully, for the Debtor to insist upon it as *true legal Payment*. Just so it is in Good Works done by the Power of God's Grace, which we could never have done without it; and therefore such cannot be *truly meritorious*.

2. What is *truly meritorious* must not be defective; because the Proportion is to be equal between the Act, and the Reward due to it; which being perfect, requires that there be no Defect in the Acts which merit it. But this can never be said of Good Works of justified Persons, that they have no Defects in them. We do not say, they are not Good Works, but they are not exact and perfect: for altho the Grace of God, as it comes from him, be a perfect Gift; yet as it acts upon Mens Minds, it doth not raise them to such a degree, but that they have Imperfections in their best Actions. And whatever is defective, is faulty; whatever is faulty, must be forgiven; whatever needs forgiveness, cannot be *truly meritorious*. But not only their Good Works are defective; but if they would merit, they ought to have none but Good Works, whereas the mixture of others renders the good uncapable of being *meritorious*, because there is so much to be pardoned, as takes away all claim of *Merit* in the good they perform. And themselves do not pretend, that Men can merit the Grace of Remission; but it is very strange that those who cannot deserve to be forgiven, should deserve to have an infinite Reward bestowed upon them.

Meritum se habet ad præmium sicut pretium ad illud quod emitur. Altisiodor. *l. 3. tr. 12.*
Absoluta æqualitas inter mercedem & meritum ponitur per modum Justitiæ commutativæ. Bell. Justif. *l. 5 c. 14.*

3. There must be an exact Proportion between the Act and the Recompence: for to merit, is to pay a Price for a thing; and in such Acts of commutative Justice, there must be an Equality of one thing with another. But what Equality can there be between the imperfect Good Works of the best Men, and the most perfect Happiness of another World, especially when that consists in the fruition of the Beatifical Vision? For what Proportion can there be between our Acts towards God, and God's Acts towards the Blessed in Heaven? Let the Acts be of what Person soever, or of what Nature soever, or from what Principle soever; as long as they are the Acts of finite imperfect Creatures, it is impossible there should be any Equality, or exact Proportion

portion between them and the Eternal Favour of God, which is the Reward promised.

4. Where Acts are *truly meritorious*, there follows an Obligation of strict Justice, to pay the Recompence due to them. But what strict Justice can there be between the Creator and his Creatures, to recompence the Service they are bound to perform; when their very Being, Power to act, Assistance in acting, and Recompence for it, are all from his Bounty and Goodness? But our Author would avoid all this, by saying, that though Good Works are *truly meritorious*; yet it is *through the Merits of Christ, and as they proceed from Grace, and through his Goodness and Promise that they are so*; *i.e.* they are truly meritorious, because it appears from all these things they neither are, nor can be meritorious. For,

(1.) How come the Merits of Christ to make Good Works *truly meritorious*? Are the Merits of Christ imputed to those Good Works? Then those Good Works must be as meritorious as Christ's own Works; which I suppose he will not assert. Or, is it that Christ hath merited the Grace whereby we may merit? But even this will not make our personal Acts truly meritorious; and the nature of Merit relates to the Acts, and not to the Power.

(2.) How comes the Power of Grace to make them *truly meritorious*; when the Power of Grace doth so much increase the Obligation on our side? If it be said, *That the state of Grace puts Men into a Capacity to merit:* we might more reasonably infer the contrary, that it puts them out of a Capacity of meriting; because the Remission of Sins, and the Favour of God, are things for which we can never make him any Recompence.

(3.) How comes a Divine Promise to make Acts truly meritorious? For God's Promise is an Act of meer Kindness, which is very different from strict Justice: and although by the Promise God binds himself to performance; yet how come those Acts to be more meritorious of Heaven, than the Acts of Repentance are of Remission of Sins? Yet none will now say, that there can be any Acts meritorious of that. Yet certainly there is as clear a promise of Pardon upon Repentance, as there is of Heaven upon Good Works: And if the Promise in the other case doth not make Repentance meritorious of Pardon; how can it make Good Works truly meritorious of Eternal Life? But notwithstanding, we do not deny God's Fidelity to his Promise may be called *Justice*; and so God, as a *Righteous Judg*, may give a *Crown of Righteousness to all that follow St. Paul's Example*, without making Good Works to be *truly meritorious*.

2 Tim. 4. 8.

VII. *Of Confession*.

WE do not charge the Church of *Rome*, that in the power of *Absolving*, they make *Gods of Men*, P. 14. as our *Misrepresenter* pretends.

2. We do not deny, *That Christ gave to the Bishops and Priests of the Catholick Church, Authority to absolve any truly penitent Sinner from his Sins,* (which he therefore needlesly proves out of Scripture) *and that such Absolution is ratified in Heaven.*

3. We are glad to find that our Author declares, *That no Man receives benefit by Absolution, without Repentance from the bottom of his Heart, and real Intention of forsaking his Sins*; P. 15. by which we hope he means more than Attrition.

But yet there are some things which stick with us, as to the Doctrine and Practice of the Church of *Rome* in this matter, which he takes no notice of.

1. That secret Confession of Sins to a Priest, is made so necessary to Salvation, that an *Anathema* is denounced against all that deny it, when they cannot deny that God doth forgive Sins upon true Contrition. For the Council of *Trent* doth say, *That Contrition, with Charity, doth reconcile a Man to God before the Sacrament of Penance be actually received.* But then it adds, *That the desire of Confession is included in Contrition*: Which is impossible to be proved by Scripture, Reason, or Antiquity. For so lately, as in the time of the *Master of the Sentences*, and *Gratian* (in the 12*th* Century) it was a very disputable Point, whether Confession to a Priest were necessary. And it is very hard for us to understand how that should become necessary to Salvation since, which was not then. Some of their own Writers confess, that some good Catholicks

Sess. 14. *Can.*5.

Sess. 14. *c.* 4.

Lomb. l. 4. Dist. 17. Grat. de Pænit. Dist. 1. c. 90. Quidam.

licks did not believe the necessity of it. I suppose the old Ca- *Greg.de Valen-*
nonists may pass for good Catholicks; and yet *Maldonat* *tiâ de Necessit.*
saith, *That all the Interpreters of the Decrees held, that there was* *Confess. c. 2.*
no Divine Precept for Confession to a Priest; and of the same *Maldonat. Op.T.*
Opinion he grants *Scotus* to have been. But he thinks *it is* *To. 2. de Pœnit.*
now declared to be Heresy, or he wishes it were. And we think it *c. 2, & 3.*
is too much already, unless there were better ground for it.

2. That an *Anathema* is denounced against those who do
not understand the words of Christ, *Whose Sins ye remit, they* John 20. 23.
are remitted, &c. of the Sacrament of Penance, so as to imply the necessity of Confession: Whereas there is no appearance in the words of any such Sense; and themselves grant,
that in order to the Remission of Sins, by Baptism, (of which
St. *Matthew* and St. *Mark* speak in the *Apostles Commission*) S. Mat. 28. 19.
there is no necessity of *Sacramental Confession*, but a general Mark 16. 16.
Confession is sufficient. And from hence the Elder *Jansenius.Concord*
us concludes, *That the Power of Remission of Sins here granted,* *Evang. c. 147*
doth not imply Sacramental Confession. *Cajetan* yields, *There is* *Cajetan. in loc.*
no Command for Confession here. And *Catharinus* adds, *That Ca-* *Ed. Paris,*
jetan would not allow any one Place of Scripture to prove Auricu- *1540.*
lar Confession. And as to this particular, he denies that there *Catharin. in Ca-*
is any Command for it; and he goes not about to prove it, *jetan. l. 5.*
but that *Cajetan* contradicts himself elsewhere, viz. when he *p. 444.*
wrote School-Divinity, before he set himself to the study of
the Scriptures. *Vasquez* saith, *That if these words may be un-* *Vasquez. in 3*
derstood of Baptism, none can infer from them the Necessity of *Part.Th.Tom.4.*
Auricular Confession. But *Gregory de Valentia* evidently proves, *Qu. 90. Art. 1.*
that this place doth relate to Remission of Sins in Baptism; *Dub.2. Num. 2.*
not only from the Comparison of Places, but from the Te- *Greg. de Va-*
stimonies of S. *Cyprian*, S. *Ambrose*, and others. *lent. in Thom.*
Tom. 4. Disp. 7.

3. That it is expressed in the same *Anathema*'s that this *Qu.9. Punct. 2.*
hath been always the Doctrine and Practice of the Catho- *p. 284.*
lick Church from the beginning. We do not deny the ancient practice, either of *Canonical Confession*, as part of the
Discipline of the Church for publick Offences; nor of *Vo-*
luntary Confession, for ease and satisfaction of the perplexed
Minds of doubting or dejected Penitents; but that which
we say was not owned nor practised by the Church from the
Beginning, was this Sacramental Confession as necessary to
the Remission of Sins before God. It is therefore to no purpose

(48)

pose to produce out of *Bellarmine*, and others, a great number of Citations, to prove that which we never deny; but if they hold to the Council of *Trent*, they must prove from the Fathers, that Sins after Baptism cannot be forgiven without Confession to Men: which those who consider what they do, will never undertake, there being so many Testimonies of undoubted Antiquity against it. And it is observable, that *Bonaventure* grants, that before the *Lateran* Decree of *Innocen.ius* 3. it was no Heresy to deny the Necessity of Confession; and so he excuses those who in the time of *Lombard* and *Gratian*, held that Opinion. And all other Christians in the World besides those of the Church of *Rome*, do to this day reject the Necessity of Particular Confession to a Priest, in order to Remission, as the Writers of the Church of *Rome* themselves confess. So *Godignus* doth of the *Abyssins*; *Philippus à SS. Trinitate*, of the *Jacobites*; *Clemens Galanus* of the *Nestorians*, who saith, *They made a Decree against the use of Confession to any but to God alone*. And *Alexius Meneses* of the Christians of S. *Thomas* in the *Indies*. The Greeks believe Confession only to be of Positive and Ecclesiastical Institution, as the late Author of the *Critical History of the Faith and Customs of the Eastern Nations*, proves. And the very Form of their Absolution declares, that they do not think particular Confession of all known Sins, necessary to Pardon: for therein the Priest absolves the Penitent from *the Sins he hath not confessed through forgetfulness, or shame*. And now let any one prove this to have been a Catholick Tradition by *Vincentius* his Rules, viz. *That it hath been always received, every where, and by All*.

Bouavent. in l. 4.Sent.Dist.17. part 2.
Godign. de rebus Abyssin. l. 1. c. 28.
Itinerarium Orientale. l. 5. c. 8.
Galan. Concil. Ecclef. Armen. Tom.2. p.605.
Historie Critiq; de la Creance & de Coutums des Nations du Levant.c.8.p.105. Ch.1. pap. 14.
Resp. 1. Jerem. Patriarch. ad Theolog.Wirtemberg. p. 87.
Arcad. de Concord. Ecclesiæ Occident. & Orient. in 7 Sacram. l. 4. c. 3.
Goar. in Euchol.og. p. 631.

VIII. *Of Indulgences*.

1. THey must be extream'y ignorant, who take the Power of Indulgences, to be *a Leave from the Pope to commit what Sins they please; and that by virtue thereof, they shall escape Punishment for their Sins, without Repentance, in another World*. Yet this is the sense of the Misrepresentation, which, he saith, is made of it. And if he saith true in his Preface, *That he hath described the Belief of a Papist, exactly according to the*

Pag. 15, 16.

appre-

apprehension he had when he was a Protestant: He shews how well he understood the Matters in difference, when I think no other Person besides himself ever had such an apprehension of it, who pretended to be any thing like a Scholar.

2. *But now he believes it damnable to hold that the Pope, or any other Power in Heaven or Earth, can give him leave to commit any Sins whatsoever ; or that for any Sum of Mony, he can obtain any Indulgence or Pardon for Sins that are to be committed by him, or his Heirs hereafter.* Very well ! But what thinks he of obtaining an Indulgence, or Pardon, after they are committed ? Is no such thing to be obtained in the Court of *Rome* for a Sum of Mony ? He cannot but have heard of the *Tax* of the *Apostolick Chamber for several Sins,* and what Sums are there set upon them. Why did he not as freely speak against this ? This is published in the vast *Collection* of *Tracts* of *Canon Law,* set forth by the *Pope's Authority,* where there are certain Rates for Perjury, Murder, Apostacy, *&c.* Now what do these *Sums* of Mony mean ? If they be small, it is so much the better Bargain, for the Sins are very great. And *Espenceus* complains, *that this Book was so far from being called in, that,* he saith, *the Pope's Legats renewed those Faculties, and confirmed them.* It seems then a Sum of Mony may be of some consequence towards the obtaining Pardon for a Sin past, tho not for a Licence to commit it. But what mighty difference is there, whether a Man procures with Mony a *Dispensation,* or a *Pardon ?* For the Sin can hurt him no more, than if he had Licence to commit it.

3. *He doth believe there is a Power in the Church to grant Indulgences.;* which, he saith, *concern not at all the Remission of Sins, either Mortal or Venial, but only of some Temporal Punishments remaining due after the Guilt is remitted.* Here now arises a Material Question, *viz.* Whether the *Popes,* or the *Representer,* be rather to be believed. If the *Popes,* who grant the Indulgences are to be believed ; then not only the bare Remission of Sins is concerned in them, but *the Plenary,* and *most Plenary Remission of Sins* is to be had by them. So *Boniface* the 8th, in his Bull of *Jubilee* granted, *Non solum, plenam & largiorem, imo plenissimam veniam peccatorum.* If these words had no relation to remission of Sins, the People were horribly cheated by the sound of them. In the Bull of *Clement* the 6th,

Tractat.Tracta-tuum. To. 15. Part.1. f.358.

Espencæ.in Ep. ad Tit.c. 1. digriss.2.

Bullar.Ghrali. i.Tom. p.204.

not extant in the *Bullarium*, but published out of the *Utrecht* Manuscript, not only a Plenary Absolution from all Sins is declared to all Persons who died in the Way to *Rome*; but he commands the Angels of Paradise to carry the Soul immediatly to Heaven. And I suppose, whatever implies such an Absolution as carries a Soul to Heaven, doth concern Remission of Sins. *Boniface* IX, granted Indulgences, *à Pœnâ & à Culpâ*; and those certainly concerned Remission of Sins; being not barely from the Temporal Punishment, but from the Guilt it self. *Clement* the 8th, whom *Bellarmine* magnifies for his care in reforming Indulgences, in his Bull of *Jubilee*, grants *a most Plenary Remission of Sins*; and *Urban* the 8th, since him, not only a Relaxation of Penances, but *Remission of Sins*; and so lately as *A. D.* 1671: *Clement* the 10th published an Indulgence upon the Canonization of five new Saints, wherein he not only grants a Plenary Indulgence of Sins, but upon invocation of one of these Saints *in the point of Death*, a Plenary Indulgence of all his Sins. And what doth this signify *in the point of Death*, if it do not concern the Remission of Sins?

Præces mittens Angelis Paradisi, quatenus animam illius à Purgatorio penitus absolutam in Paradisi gloriam introducant.
Bull. Clem. 6. ultra-jecti A. D. 1653.
Gobat. Person. Cosmodr. et. 6. c. 85. p.278.
Bullar. To. 3. p.74. To.4. p.86.

4. Indulgences, he saith, *are nothing else but a Mitigation or Relaxation, upon just Causes, of Canonical Penances, which are or may be enjoyned by the Pastors of the Church on penitent Sinners, according to their several degrees of Demerits.* If by Canonical Penances, they mean those enjoined by the Penitential Canons, *Greg. de Valentia* saith, *This Opinion differs not from that of the Hereticks, and makes Indulgences to be useless and dangerous things.* *Bellarmine* brings several Arguments against this Doctrine. (1.) *There would be no need of the Treasure of the Church*; which he had proved to be the Foundation of Indulgences. (2.) *They would be rather hurtful than profitable, and the Church would deceive her Children by them.* (3.) *They could not be granted for the Dead.* (4.) *They who receive Indulgences, do undergo Canonical Penances.* (5.) *The Form of them doth express, that they do relate to God, and not only to the Church.* And this, I think, is sufficient to shew how far he is from true Representing the Nature of Indulgences; for we do not dispute the Church's Power in relaxing Canonical Penances to Penitent Sinners upon just Causes.

Greg. de Valent. de Indulg. c. 2.
Bell. de Indulg. l.1. c.7.

C. 2.

IX. Of Satisfaction.

1. HE believes it damnable to think any thing injuriously of Christ's Passion: But then he distinguishes *the Eternal and Temporal Pain due to Sin.* *As to the Guilt and Eternal Pain, the Satisfaction,* he saith, *is proper to Christ ; but as to the Temporal Pain, which may remain due by God's Justice, after the other are remitted,* he saith, *that Penitent Sinners may in some measure satisfy for that by Prayer, Fasting, Alms, &c.* p. 17.

2. *These Penitential Works,* he saith, *are no otherwise satisfactory, than as joined and applied to Christ's Satisfaction, in virtue of which alone our good Works find a grateful acceptance in God's sight.* p. 19.

But for right apprehending the State of the Controversy, we must consider ;

1. That they grant both Eternal and Temporal Pain due to Sin, to be remitted in Baptism ; so that all the Satisfaction to be made, is for Sins committed after Baptism.

2. We distinguish between Satisfaction to the Church before Absolution, and Satisfaction to the Justice of God for some part of the punishment to Sin which is unremitted.

3. We do not deny that truly Penitential Works are pleasing to God, so as to avert his Displeasure ; but we deny that there can be *any Compensation in way of equivalency,* between what we suffer, and what we deserve.

Catech. Roman. Part. 2. c. 5. n. 52, 56.

The Matter in Controversy therefore on this Head, consists in these things.

1. That after the total Remission of Sins in Baptism, they suppose a Temporal Punishment to remain, when the Eternal is forgiven ; which the Penitent is to satisfy God's Justice for ; and without this being done in this Life, he must go into Purgatory for that End. Of which more under that Head.

2. That this Satisfaction may be made to the Justice of God, after Absolution is given by the Priest. So that altho the Penitent be admitted into God's Favour, by the Power of the Keys, according to their own Doctrine ; yet the Application of the Merits of Christ, together with the Saints

in the Sentence of Abfolution (according to their Form) do not fet him fo free, but he either wants a new Supply from the Treafure of the Church, *i. e.* from the fame Merits of Chrift and the Saints; or elfe he is to fatisfy for the Temporal Punifhment by his own Penances.

3. That thefe Penitential Works are to be joined with the Merits of Chrift, in the way of proper Satisfaction to Divine Juftice. And however foftly this may be expreffed; the meaning is, that Chrift hath merited, that we may merit, and by his Satisfaction, we are enabled to fatisfy for our felves. And if the Satisfaction by way of Juftice be taken away, the other will be a Controverfy about Words.

Catten. Rom. de Pænit. Sacr. n. 51.

4. That thefe Penitential Works may not only be fufficient for themfelves, but they may be fo over-done, that a great fhare may be taken from them to make up the Treafure of the Church, for the benefit of others who fall fhort, when they are duly applied to them in the way of Indulgences. And about thefe Points, we muft defire greater Proof than we have ever yet feen.

X. *Of reading the Holy Scripture.*

Pag. 15.

1. HE believes it damnable in any one, to think, fpeak, or do any thing irreverently towards the Scripture, or by any means whatfoever to bring it into difrepute or difgrace: but not being contented with this, he adds, *That he holds it in the higheft Veneration of all Men living.* Now, here we muft defire a little better Reprefentation of this Matter. For certainly, thofe who derive its Authority from the Church; who fet Traditions in equal efteem with it; who complain fo much of its Obfcurity, can never be faid to hold it in equal Veneration with thofe who maintain its independent Authority, its Sufficiency, and Perfpicuity. And thefe are known and material Points in Controverfy between us and them: therefore let them not fay, they hold it in the higheft Veneration of all Men living; tho thofe thought themfelves through Catholicks, who have compared it to a *Nofe of Wax, to a* Lefbian *Rule, to a dead Letter, unfenfed Characters,* and to other things, not fit to be repeated. But we are well pleafed to find

find them express such Veneration for it. Wherefore then are the People to be kept from reading it?

2. He saith, *It is not out of disrespect to it.* But why then? (1.) *Because private Interpretation is not proper for the Scripture*, (2 Pet. 1. 20.) One would think the Scripture were not kept *only* from the People, by such a Sense being put upon it; for any one that would but consider that place, will find it must relate to the Prophets themselves; and doth he think the Prophets were to be debarred from reading the Scriptures? But this is playing with Scripture, and not reasoning from it. (2.) *Because in the Epistles of S. Paul are certain things hard to be understood, which the unlearned and unstable deprave, as also the rest of the Scriptures, to their own Perdition,* (2 Pet. 3. 16.) Now in my Opinion, such Men deserve more to be debarred from medling with the Scripture, who make such perverse Inferences from it, than ordinary Readers. And if they use all other places, as they do this, they cannot be excused from *depraving* it. It is granted, there were then *unlearned and unstable Men*, who misunderstood, or misapplied the Writings of St. *Paul*, and other Scriptures. And what then? There are Men of all Ages, who abuse the best things in the World, even the Gospel it self, and the Grace of God. Doth it hence follow, that the Gospel must not be preached to them, or the Grace of God made known to them, for fear of Mens making ill use of it? If this had been the just Consequence, would not St. *Peter* himself have thought of this? But he was so far from making it, that he adviseth those Persons he writes to, to have a mighty regard to the Scriptures, even to the Prophetical Writings, *is to a Light shining in a dark place*, 1 Pet. 1. 19. According to this way of deducing Consequences, S. *Peter* should have argued just contrary; *The Prophetical Writings are dark and obscure, therefore meddle not with them, but trust your Guides:* Whereas the Apostle, after he had told them what the Apostles saw and heard, he adds, *That they have a more sure Prophetical Word*, as the Rhemists translate it. How could that be *more sure* to them, unless they were allowed to read, consider, and make use of it? (3.) *Because God hath given only some to be Apostles, some Prophets, other some Evangelists, and other some Pastors and Doctors,* Ephes. 4. 11. Doth it hence follow that the People are not to read the Scriptures? In the

H Univer-

Universities, Tutors are appointed to interpret *Aristotle* to their Pupils; doth it hence follow that they are not to read *Aristotle* themselves? It is, no doubt, a mighty Advantage to have such Infallible Interpreters as the *Apostles and Prophets*; and all Christians are bound to follow their Sense, where they have delivered it. But suppose the Question be about the Sense of these Interpreters; must their Books not be looked into, because of the danger of Error? This Reason will still hold against those who go about to deliver their Sense; and so on, till by this Method of Reasoning, all sort of Books and Interpretations be rejected; unless any such can be found out, which is not liable to be abused or misunderstood. And if there be any such to be had, they are much to blame who do not discover it. But as yet we see no Remedy for two things in Mankind, a proneness to Sin, and to Mistake. But of all things, we ought not to take away from them one of the best Means to prevent both, *viz.* a diligent, and careful, and humble reading the Holy Scriptures.

But, 3. he denies *that all Persons are forbid to read the Scriptures, but only such as have no Licenfe, and good Testimony from their Curats: and therefore their design is not to preserve Ignorance in the People, but to prevent a blind, ignorant presumption.*

These are plausible Pretences to such as search no farther; but the Mystery of this Matter lies much deeper. It was, no doubt, the Design of the Church of *Rome* to keep the Bible wholly out of the hands of the People. But upon the Reformation they found it impossible; so many Translations being made into vulgar Languages; and therefore care was taken to have Translations made by some of their own Body; and since the People of better inclinations to Piety were not to be satisfied without the Bible; therefore they thought it the better way to permit certain Persons whom they could trust, to have a Licence to read it: And this was the true Reason of the Fourth Rule of the *Index Liber. prohibit.* made in pursuance of the Order of the Council of *Trent*, and published by *Pius* IV. by which any one may see it was not an Original Permission out of any good Will to the Thing; but an Aftergame to get the Bible out of the Hands of the People again: And therefore Absolution was to be denied to those who would not deliver them to their Ordinaries when they were called for:

for: And the Regulars themselves were not to be permitted to have Bibles without a Licenſe: And as far as I can underſtand the Addition of *Clement* VIII, to that Fourth Rule, he withdraws any new Power of granting ſuch Licenſes; and ſaith they are contrary to the *Command and Uſage of that Church, which*, he ſaith, *is to be inviolably obſerved:* Wherein I think he declares himſelf fully againſt ſuch Licenſes: And that Inferior Guides ſhould grant them againſt the Command of the Head of the Church, is a thing not very agreeable to the Unity and Subordination they boaſt of.

Quod quidem inviolatè ſervandum eſt. Clem. VIII. ad Reg. 4. Indicis Roman.

XI. *Of Apocryphal Books.*

1. WE do not charge the Church of *Rome* with *making what Additions to Scripture they think good*, as the *Miſrepreſenter* ſaith; but we charge them with taking into the Canon of Scripture ſuch Books as were not received for Canonical by the Chriſtian Church; as thoſe Books himſelf mentions, *viz. Toby, Judith, Eccleſiaſticus, Wiſdom*, and *Maccabees*.

p. 21.

2. We do not only charge them with this, but with Anathematizing all thoſe who do not upon this Declaration believe them to be Canonical; ſince they cannot but know, that theſe Books never were in the *Jewiſh* Canon, and were left out by many Chriſtian Writers. And if the Church cannot add to the Scripture, and our Author *thinks it damnable to do it*; how can it make any Books *Canonical*, which were not ſo received by the Church? For the *Scripture* in this ſenſe is the *Canon*; and therefore if it add to the *Canon*, it adds to the Scripture; *i.e.* it makes it neceſſary to believe ſome Books to be of infallible Authority, which were not believed to be ſo, either by the *Jewiſh* or Chriſtian Church, as appears by abundant Teſtimonies to that purpoſe produced by a Learned Biſhop of this Church; which ought to have been conſidered by the *Repreſenter*, that he might not have talked ſo crudely about this Matter.

Concil. Trident. Seſſ.4.8. Apr. de Canon. Script.

Bp *Coſins* Scholaſtical Hiſtory of the Canon of Scripture.

But however, I muſt conſider what he ſaith;

1. He produces the Teſtimony of *Greg. Nazianzen*, who is expreſly againſt him, and declares but Twenty two Books in the Canon of the Old Teſtament; but how doth he prove

Greg. Nazianzen. in *Carmin*, 2 *Vol. p.* 98.

(56)

prove that he thought these Books Canonical? He quotes his *Oration on the Maccabees*; where I can find nothing like it; and instead of it he expresly follows, as he declares, the Book of *Josephus*, of *the Authority of Reason* concerning them. So that if this proves any thing, it proves *Josephus* his Book Canonical, and not the *Maccabees*.

_{Orat. de Mac-
cab. vol. 1.
p. 358.}

2. He adds the Testimony of St. *Ambrose*, who in the place he refers to, enlarges on the Story of the *Maccabees*, but saith nothing of the Authority of the Book. And even *Coccius* himself grants, that of old *Melito Sardensis*, *Amphilochius*, *Greg. Nazienzen*, the Council of *Laodicea*, St. *Hierom*, *Ruffinus*, and *Gregory* the Great, did not own the Book of *Maccabees* for Canonical.

_{Ambros. de Ja-
cob. & Vitæ E-
rat. l. 2. c. 10,
11, 12.
Cocci. Thes. Ca-
thol. l. 5. Act. 18}

3. *Innocentius ad Exuperium* speaks more to his purpose. And if that Decretal Epistle be allowed, against which Bishop *Cosins* hath made considerable Objections; then it must be granted, that these Books were then in the *Roman* Canon; but that they were not received by the Universal Church, appears evidently by the Canon of the Council of *Laodicea*, c. 60. wherein these Books are left out; and this was received in the Code of the Universal Church; which was as clear a Proof of the Canon then generally received, as can be expected. It is true, the Council of *Carthage* took them in; and St. *Augustine* seems to be of the same Opinion: But on the other side, they are left out by *Melito* Bishop of *Sardis*, who lived near the Apostles times, *Origen*, *Athanasius*, S. *Hilary*, St. *Cyril* of *Jerusalem*, *Epiphanius*, St. *Basil*, *Amphilochius*, St. *Chrysostom*, and especially St. *Jerom*, who hath laboured in this point so much, that no fewer than thirteen places are produced out of him to this purpose, by the fore-mentioned Learned Bishop of our Church, who clearly proves there was no Tradition for the Canon of the Council of *Trent* in any one Age of the Christian Church. But our Author goes on.

_{Scholastical Hi-
story, n. 83.}

_{Euseb. l. 5. c. 24.
Orig. Præf. in
Psal.
Athan. in Sy-
nopsi.
Hilar. præf. in
Psal.
S. Cyril. Ca-
tech. 4.
Epiph. hær. 8. 76
Basil. Philocal.
c. 3.
Amphil. Epist.
Canon. ad Se-
leuc.
Chrys. hom. 4. in
Gen.
Scholast. Hist.
n. 71.
P. 22.}

4. *It is of little concern to him, whether these Books were ever in the Hebrew Copy.* I would only ask whether it be of any concern to him, whether they were divinely inspired or not? He saith, *It is damnable to add to the Scripture*; by the Scripture we mean Books written by Divine Inspiration: Can the Church make Books to be so written, which were not so written? If not, then all it hath to do, is to deliver by Tradition what
was

was so, and what not. Whence should they have this Tradition, but from the *Jews?* and they owned no Divine Inspiration after the time of *Malachy*. How then should there be any Books so written after that time? And he that saith in this Matter, as he doth, *It is of little concern to him whether they were in the Hebrew Canon*, doth little concern himself what he ought to believe, and what not, in this matter.

5. Since the Churches Declaration, he saith, *no Catholicks ever doubted.* What doth he mean by the Churches Declaration, that of *Innocent*, and the Council of *Carthage?* Then the same Bishop hath shewed him, that since that time, there have been very many, both in the *Greek* and *Latin* Church, of another Opinion. And a little before the Council of *Trent*, *Catharinus* saith, *That a Friend of his, and a Brother in Christ, derided him as one that wanted Learning, for daring to assert these Books were within the Canon of Scripture;* and it is plain, *Card. Cajetan* could never be perswaded of it: But if he means since the Council of *Trent*, then we are returned to our Difficulty, how such a Council can make any Books Canonical, which were not received for such by the Catholick Church before? For then they do not declare the Canon, but create it.

P. 23.

Cathar. Adver. Cajet. p. 48. ed. Paris 1535.

XII. *Of the Vulgar Edition of the Bible.*

1. WE do not dispute about the *Vulgar Edition*, whether it may not be preferr'd before modern *Latin* Editions, because of its great *Antiquity* in some parts of it, and its general Reception since the time of *Gregory* I: But our dispute is, whether it be made so *Authentick* since the Council of *Trent*, that no Appeals are to be made to the Originals, *i. e.* whether that Council by its Authority could make a Version equal to the Originals out of which it was made? Especially since at the time of that Decree, the Vulgar Edition was confessed to be full of Errors and Corruptions by *Sixtus* V. who saith, he took infinite pains to correct them, and yet left very many behind, as appeared by *Clement* VIII. who corrected his *Bibles* in very many places, and grants some faults were left uncorrected still: Now, how

P. 24, 25.

In hac Vulgata Editione visa sunt nonnulla mutanda, quæ consulto mutata non sunt. Clem. VIII. in Bulla.

was

was it possible for the Council of *Trent* to declare that Edition Authentick, which was afterwards so much corrected? And, whether was the correct Edition of *Sixtus* V. *Authentick*, or not, being made in pursuance of the Decree of the Council? If not, how comes *Clement* his Edition to be made Authentick, when the other was not, since there may be Corruptions found in that, as well as the other; and no one can tell, but it may be reviewed and corrected still; as some of their own Writers confess *it stands in need of it*?

<small>Luc. Brugens. *in variis Lect.*</small>

2. Our Controversy is not so much about the Authority of the Vulgar *Latin*, above other *Latin* Versions to those who understand them; but whether none else but the *Latin* Version must be used by those who understand it not? And here our *Representer* saith, *That he is commanded not to read any of these Translations* (speaking of *Tindal's*, and that in Q. *Elizabeth's time*) *but only that which is recommended to him by the Church*. If this relate to the *Vulgar Latin*, then we are to seek, why the common People should have none to read, but what they cannot understand; if to *Translations of their own*, then we doubt not to make it appear, that our Translation allowed among us, is more exact and agreeable than any they can put into their hands.

<small>Nat. Alexand. *dissert de vulg. vers. quæst. 6.*</small>

<small>P. 26.</small>

XIII. *Of the Scriptures as a Rule of Faith.*

<small>P. 27.</small>

THE only thing insisted on here is, *That it is not the Words, but the Sense of Scripture is the Rule; and that this Sense is not to be taken from Mens private Fancies, which are various and uncertain; and therefore where there is no security from Errors, there is nothing capable of being a Rule.*

To clear this, we must consider,

1. That it is not necessary to the making of a Rule, to prevent any possibility of mistake, but that it be such that they cannot mistake without their own fault. For Certainty in it self, and Sufficiency for the use of others, are all the necessary Properties of a Rule; but after all, it's possible for Men not to apply the Rule aright, and then they are to be blamed, and not the Rule.

2. If no Men can be certain of the right Sense of Scripture,

ture, then it is not plain in neceſſary things; which is contrary to the deſign of it, and to the cleareſt Teſtimonies of Antiquity, and to the common ſenſe of all Chriſtians, who never doubted or diſputed the Senſe of ſome things revealed therein; as the Unity of the Godhead, the making of the World by him, the Deluge, the Hiſtory of the Patriarchs, the Captivity of the Jews, the coming of the Meſſias, his ſending his Apoſtles, his coming again to Judgment, &c. No Man who reads ſuch things in Scripture, can have any doubt about the ſenſe and meaning of the Words.

3. Where the Senſe is dubious, we do not allow any Man to put what Senſe he pleaſes upon them; but we ſay, there are certain means, whereby he may either attain to the true Senſe, or not be damned if he do not. And the firſt thing every Man is to regard, is not his ſecurity from being deceived, but from being damned. For Truth is made known in order to Salvation: If therefore I am ſure to attain the chief end, I am not ſo much concerned, as to the poſſibility of Errors, as that I be not deceived by my own fault. We do not therefore leave Men *either to follow their own fancy, or to interpret Scripture by it*; but we ſay, They are bound upon pain of Damnation to ſeek the Truth ſincerely, and to uſe the beſt means in order to it; and if they do this, they either will not err, or their Errors will not be their Crime.

XIV. *Of the Interpretation of Scripture.*

1. THE Queſtion is not, Whether Men are not bound to make uſe of the beſt means for the right Interpretation of Scripture, by Reading, Meditation, Prayer, Advice, a humble and teachable Temper, &c. *i. e.* all the proper means fit for ſuch an end? but whether after all theſe, there be a neceſſity of ſubmitting to ſome Infallible Judg. in order to the attaining the certain Senſe of Scripture?

2. The Queſtion is not, Whether we ought not to have a mighty regard to the Senſe of the whole Chriſtian Church in all Ages ſince the Apoſtles, which we profeſs to have; but, Whether the *preſent Roman Church*, as it ſtands divided from other Communions, hath ſuch a Right and Authority to interpret

pret Scripture, that we are bound to believe that to be the Infallible Sense of Scripture which she delivers?

And here I cannot but take notice how strangely this matter is here misrepresented: for the Case is put,

P. 29.   1. *As if every one who rejects their pretence of Infallibility, had nothing to guide him but his own private Fancy in the Interpretation of Scripture.*

2. *As if we rejected the Sense put upon Scripture by the whole Community of Christians in all Ages since the Apostles times.* Whereas we appeal in the matters in difference between us, to this universal Sense of the Christian Church, and are verily perswaded they cannot make it out in any one Point wherein we differ from them. And themselves cannot deny, that in several we have plainly the consent of the first Ages, as far as appears by the Books remaining, on our side; as in the Worship of Images, Invocation of Saints, Papal Supremacy, Communion in both kinds, Prayer and Scripture in known Tongues; and I may safely add, the Sufficiency of the Scripture, Transubstantiation, Auricular Confession, Publick Communions, Solitary Masses, to name no more.

But here lies the Artifice; We must not pretend to be capable of judging either of Scripture, or Tradition; but we must trust their Judgment what is the sense of Scripture, and what hath been the Practice of the Church in all Ages, altho their own Writers confess the contrary: which is very hard.

But he seems to argue for such a submission to the Church;
1. *Because we receive the Book of Scripture from her; therefore from her we are to receive the sense of the Book.* An admirable Argument!
P. 29.   We receive the *Old Testament* from the *Jews*; therefore from them we are to receive the sense of the *Old Testament*, and so we are to reject the true *Messias*. But this is not all: If by the Church, they mean the Church of *Rome* in distinction from others, we deny it: if they mean the whole Christian Church, we grant it; but then the force of it is quite lost. But why is it not possible for the Church of *Rome* to keep these Writings, and deliver them to others, which make against her self? Do not Persons in Law-Suits often produce Deeds which make against them? But there is yet a further Reason; it was not possible for the Church of *Rome* to make away these *Writings*, being so universally spread.

2. Be-

2. *Because the Church puts the difference between true and false Books, therefore that must be trusted for the true sense of them.* Which is just as if one should argue, The Clerks of the Rolls are to give an account to the Court of true Records, therefore they are to sit on the Bench, and to give Judgment in all Causes. The Church is only to declare what it finds as to Canonical Books; but hath no Power to make any Book Canonical which was not before received for such. But I confess *Stapleton* saith, the Church if it please may make *Hermes* his Pastor, and *Clemens* his Constitutions Canonical: but I do not think our Author will therein follow him.

Controv. 5.
Qu. 4. art. 2.

XV. *Of Tradition.*

1. THE Question is not about *Human Traditions supplying the Defects of Scripture*, as he misrepresents it; but whether there be an unwritten word, which we are equally bound to receive with the Written word: Altho these things which pass under that Name, are really but *Humane Traditions*; yet we do not deny that they pretend them to be of Divine Original.

P. 30, 31.

2. We do not deny, but the '*Apostles might deliver such things by Word as well as by Epistle, which their Disciples were bound to believe and keep*: but we think there is some difference to be made between what we certainly know they delivered in Writing, and what it is now impossible for us to know; *viz.* what they delivered by word without writing.

2 Thes. 2. 13.

3. We see no ground why any one should believe any Doctrine *with a stedfast and Divine Faith*, which is not bottom'd on the Written word; for then his Faith must be built on the Testimony of the Church as Divine and Infallible, or else his Faith cannot be Divine. But it is impossible to prove it to be Divine and Infallible, but by the Written word; and therefore, as it is not reasonable that he should believe the Written word by such a Divine Testimony of the Church; so if any particular Doctrine may be received on the Authority of the Church without the Written word, then all Articles of Faith may, and so there would be no need of the Written word.

P. 31.

4. The

P. 32.   4. *The Faith of Christians doth no otherwise stand upon the Foundation of the Churches Tradition*, than as it delivers down to us the Books of Scripture; but we acknowledg the general Sense of the Christian Church to be a very great help for understanding the true sense of Scripture; and we do not reject any thing so delivered; but what is all this to the Church of *Rome*? But this is still the way of true Representing.

XVI. *Of Councils.*

P. 33.   1. WE are glad to find so good a Resolution as seems to be expressed in these words, viz. *That he is obliged to believe nothing besides that which Christ taught, and his Apostles; and if any thing contrary to this should be defined, and commanded to be believed, even by Ten Thousand Councils, he believes it damnable in any one to receive it, and by such Decrees to make Additions to his Creed.* This seems to be a very good saying, and it is pity any thing else should overthrow it. But here lies the Misrepresenting; he will believe what Christ and his Apostles taught, from the Definitions of Councils, and so all this goodly Fabrick falls to nothing; for it is but as if one should say, If *Aristotle* should falsly deliver *Plato*'s sense, I will never believe him, but I am resolved to take *Plato*'s sense only from *Aristotle*'s words. So here, he first declares he will take the Faith of Christ from the Church; and then he saith, if the Church Representative should contradict the Faith of Christ, he would never believe it.

2. We dispute not with them, the Right and Necessity of *General Councils* (upon great occasions) if they be truly so, rightfully called, lawfully assembled, and fairly managed; which have been, and may be of great use to the Christian world, for setling the Faith, healing the Breaches of Christendom, and reforming Abuses. And we farther say that the Decrees of such Councils ought to be submitted to, where they proceed upon certain Grounds of Faith, and not upon unwritten Traditions; Which was the fatal stumbling at the Threshold in the Council of *Trent*, and was not to be recovered afterwards; for their setting up Traditions equally with the written VVord, made it easie

for

for them to define, and as easie for all others to reject their Definitions, in case there had not been so many other Objections against the Proceedings of that Council. And so all our Dispute concerning this matter is taken off from the general Notion, and runs into the particular Debate concerning the Qualifications and Proceedings of some which were called Free, General Councils; but were neither *General*, nor *Free*; and therefore *could not deliver the sense of the Catholick Church*, which our Author requires them to do.

P. 33.

XVII. *Of Infallibility in the Church.*

1. HE doth not pretend this belongs *to the Pastors and Prelates of his Church, who may fall*, he saith, *into Heresie and Schism; but that the whole Church is secured by Divine Promises from all Error and Danger of Prevarication*; which he proves from the Promises of the New Testament, Mat. 16. 18 —— 28. 20. *John* 14. 16, 26. But however the former seems to take away Infallibility from the Guides of the Church, yet that this is to be understood of them *separately*, appears by what follows.

P. 36.

2. *The like Assistance of the Holy Ghost he believes to be in all General Councils, which is the Church Representative; by which they are specially protected from all error in all definitions and declarations in matters of Faith.*

P. 38.

Now here are two sorts of Infallibility tacked to one another by vertue of these general Promises, which ought more distinctly to be considered.

1. To preserve Chrifts Church so as it shall never cease to be a Church, is one thing; to preserve it from all Error is another: The former answers the End of Christs Promises as to the *Duration* of the *Church*; and the latter is not implied in them.

2. The promise of *teaching them all Truth*, Joh. 16. 13. is not made to the whole Church, but to the *Apostles*: And their case was so peculiar and extraordinary, that there can be no just inference from the assistance promised to them, of what the Church would enjoy in all Ages.

3. If the diffusive Church have no infallible Assistance promised, then no infallible Assistance can from thence be proved

I 2

for

for the Church Reprefentative ; fo that fome particular Promifes to the Guides of the Church as affembled together, are neceffary to prove the Infallibility of Councils.

P. 38.   4. It by no means proves following Councils to be Infallible, becaufe the Apoftles faid, *Acts* 15. 28. *It feemed good to the Holy Ghoft, and to us.* Our Author *doth not doubt, but the fame may be prefixed to all determinations in point of Faith, refolved on by any General Council lawfully affembled fince that time, or to be held to the Worlds end.* But what Reafon he had for not doubting in this matter, I cannot fee ; the *Affiftance*, he faith, *being to extend as far as the Promife :* But fhall *Affiftance* imply *Infallibility ?* Then there muft be good ftore, as long as the Promifes of Divine Grace hold good : But this Affiftance of Councils is very different from the Affiftance of Grace, for the Church may fubfift without Councils, but cannot without Grace : VVhat General Council was there from the meeting, *Acts* 15. to the Council of *Nice ?* VVere not Chrifts Promifes fulfilled to his Church all that time, when it encreafed in all parts againft the moft violent Oppofition ?

5. No Parity of Reafon from the *Jewifh* Church can be fufficient Proof for Infallibility in the Chriftian. But our Author

P. 39.   argues thus, *If Gods fpecial Affiftance was never wanting to the Church of the Jews fo as to let it fail in the truth of its Doctrine, or its Authority ; Why fhould not we believe the fame of the Church of Chrift, which is built on better Promifes ?* VVhat fpecial Affiftance was it which *Ifrael* had, when it is faid, that *for a long time* Ifrael

2 Chron. 15 3. *had been without the true God, and without a teaching Prieft, and without Law ?* And as to *Judah*, was there no failing in point of Doctrine in our Saviours time ? It is true they had the Law intire, and that was all that was good among them, for their Teachers had corrupted themfelves and the People, and made the Law of no effect among them : If there were Infallibility any where, it muft be in the high Prieft and *Sanhedrim* ; but is it poffible for any Chriftian to think them Infallible when they were fo grofly miftaken about the main Article of their Faith as to the Meffias, and pronounced him worthy of death ? Is not this a fine Argument for the Infallibility of the Guides of the Chriftian Church ? *But the Church of Chrift hath better Promifes:*

No

No doubt of it, greater Promises of Grace and Mercy in this World, and in that to come: but what is all this to Infallibility in Councils?

6. Christ's Command of Obedience to those who sat in *Moses* Chair, (*Matt.* 23. 2.) doth not prove the Infallibility of those who sat there. Yet this is alledged to that purpose; and that men ought not to doubt of the reasonableness of the Commands of their Superiors. But St. *Chrysostom* saith, *our Saviour speaks of the things commanded by the Law of* Moses. *Per Cathedram Doctrinam Legis ostendit,* saith St. *Jerom*: *Not their own Doctrine, but that of* Moses, saith *Isidore*; and so *Hilary* and *Theophylact*. *Maldonate* confesseth, our Saviours Words are to be understood, not of their own Doctrine, but of that of the Law; and therefore he yields the Obedience here required to be restrained to that; *All things,* saith *Cajetan, which they teach out of* Moses's *Chair*: *Not all their Doctrines, but as far as they were conformable to the Laws,* saith *Ferus*. Now can any one hence infer, that no men ought to dispute any Commands of Superiors, when it is supposed, that there is a Rule and Standard for them to speak according to; and our Saviour elsewhere doth suppose these very Men to teach things contrary to the Law; as in the Case of *Corban.* Would our Saviour contradict himself? or require a blind Obedience in things repugnant to the Law? We do not deny a due submission to our Superiours in the Church; yea, we allow them a Power to determine things not forbidden; and think Obedience due in such things by vertue of their Authority; but yet this is far enough from Infallibility, or an unlimited implicit Obedience, which would overthrow the force of all our Saviours Reasonings against the *Scribes* and *Pharisees,* as to their misinterpreting the Law, and the Superstitious Practises they imposed upon the People.

p. 29.
Chrysost. in *Mat. Hom.* 72.
Hieron. in loc.
Caten. Gr. in loc.
Hilar. Canon. 24.
Theophilact. in loc.

Matt. 15.

XVIII. *Of the* POPE.

1. WE do not charge them with *believing the Pope to be God*; which it seems himself did, if we believe the *Misrepresenter* in his Preface; but there is some Reason to doubt whether

_{Cerem. Sect. 1.}
_{c. 2.} ther they do not at some times give him greater Honour than becomes a Man. I instance in the Adoration after his Election, when the new Pope is placed upon the Altar to receive the Submissions of the Cardinals: but the Altar, themselves do confess to be sacred to God alone: And there they profess to Worship Jesus Christ, as present in the Host. This therefore looks too much like assuming the Place of Christ, and not becoming the Distance between God and Man.

_{P. 40.} 2. The Question is, *Whether Christ hath appointed the Pope or Bishop of Rome to be Pastor, Governour, and Head of his Church under him?* This, he saith, *he believes,* and this he knows we deny; and therefore had Reason to expect some Proof of it. But instead thereof he tells us *how they look on themselves as obliged to shew him the Respect due to his Place,* which he knows is not the matter in Question. Two things however he saith, which seem to justifie his Title.

_{P. 41.} 1. *He is the Successor of St.* Peter, *to whom Christ committed the care of his Flock.* But how far is this from proving the Pope to be Head of the Church under Christ? For how doth it appear that Christ ever made St. *Peter* Head of the Church, or committed his Flock to him, in contradistinction to the rest of the Apostles? This is so far from being evident from Scripture, that the Learned Men of their Church are ashamed of the Places commonly produced for it; it being impossible ever to justifie the sense of them according to their own Rules of interpreting Scripture, *viz.* by the unanimous consent
_{Matt. 16. 18.} of the Fathers. For, 1. *Thou art Peter, and upon this Rock will*
_{Chrysost. hom.} *I build my Church,* is interpreted by many of the Fathers both
_{1. in Pentec.} Greek and *Latin,* of S. *Peters* Confession, and not of his Person;
_{Tom. 5. ed} so by S. *Chrysostom,* S. *Ambrose,* S. *Augustin,* S. *Basil* of *Seluciæ,*
_{Savil. p. 979.} S. *Hilary,* S. *Gregory Nyssen,* and *Theodoret;* all great and consi-
_{Ambros. de} derable Persons in the Christian Church, whose Words are plain
_{Incarnat. dom.} and full to that purpose; and so they can never produce the una-
_{Sacramento} nimous consent of the Fathers for S. *Peter's* Supremacy out of
_{c. 5. Aug. de} these words. 2. *And unto thee will I give the Keys of the Kingdom*
_{verbis Dom.} *of Heaven,* are interpreted by the Fathers of S. *Peter* in common
_{ad Evang. se-}
_{cund. Matth.}
_{Serm. 13.}
_{Tract in Joh. 124. Basil. Seleuc. Orat. 25. ad fin. Hilar. de Trinit. l. 6. Greg. Nyssen. de Advent Domini cap. ult. Theodoret Epist. 77. 146. Matt. 16. 19.}

with

with the other Apostles; so *Origen*, S. *Cyprian*, S. *Hilary*, S. *Hierom*, and S. *Augustin*, as they are all owned by some Members of the *Roman* Communion. And 3. For these Words, *Feed my sheep*, a late Learned Doctor of the *Sorbon* shews, that if they prove any thing peculiar to S. *Peter*, they must prove him sole Pastor of the Church, which was the thing S. *Gregory* disputed against so warmly. But that there was nothing peculiar to S. *Peter*, above or beyond the rest of the Apostles, he shews at large from S. *Chrysostom*, S. *Cyril*, S. *Augustin*, and others, to whom I refer the Reader, and to the former Authors. But suppose it were made to appear, *that S. Peter was Head of the Church*, How doth the Bishop of *Rome*'s Succession in that Headship shew it self? To that he saith, 2 *That there hath been a visible succession of above Two hundred and fifty Bishops, acknowledged as such in all past Ages by the Christian World*. *As such*: What is that? As Bishops of *Rome*? That is not of weight enough to put it upon Trial; as Heads of the *Catholick Church*? That he knows is not only denied by us, but by all the *Greek*, *Armenian*, *Nestorian*, *Abyssin* Churches; so that we dare say, it was never allowed in any one Age of the Christian Church: but we need not insist on the proof of this, since the late mentioned Authors of the *Roman* Communion have taken so great pains, not only to prove the Popes Supremacy to be an Incroachment and Usurpation in the Church, but that the laying it aside is necessary to the Peace and unity of it. And until the Divine Institution of the Papal Supremacy be proved, it is to no purpose to debate *what manner of Assistance is promised to the Pope in his Decrees*. Our Author is willing to decline the debate about his *personal Infallibility*, as a matter of *Opinion*, and not of *Faith*; and yet he saith, *he doubts not but God doth grant a special Assistance to the High Priest, for the good of the whole Flock, under the New Law, as he did under the Old*, and produces the Instance of Caiaphas, Joh. 11. 51. This is a very surprizing way of Reasoning; for if his Arguments be good from Scripture, he must hold the Popes *personal Infallibility as a matter of Faith*; and yet one would hardly think he should build an Article of Faith on the Instance of *Caiaphas*: For what consequence can be drawn from Gods over-ruling the mind of a very bad man, when he was carrying on a most wicked design, to utter such words,
which

Orig. Comment. in Matt. Gr.Lat.p 275. Cyptian. de Unit.Ecclesiæ. Hilar. de Trinit. l. 6 Hier. c. Jovin. l. 1 c. 14, in Matt. 16. Aug. in Joh. Tr. 118. 124. In Epist. Joh. To 10. Moyens surs & honestes, &c. p.34. &c. Entretiens de Philaleth. & Phileren. p. 121. Joh. Launoi.Epist. part 5. Reim. Formentino, & Part. 2 Ep. 5. P. 47, &c.

P. 42.

which in the event proved true in another sense than he meant them, that therefore God will give a special Assistance to the Pope in determining matters of Faith? Was not *Caiaphas* himself the man who proposed the taking away the Life of Christ at that time? Was he assisted in that Council? Did not he determine afterwards Christ to be guilty of blasphemy, and therefore worthy of Death? And is not this a rare Infallibility which is supposed to be consistent with a Decree to crucifie Christ? And doth he in earnest think such Orders are to be obeyed, whether the supreme Pastor be infallible or not? For so he concludes, *That his Sentence is to be obeyed, whether he be Infallible or no.*

XIX. *Of Dispensations.*

HERE the *Misrepresenter* saith, That a Papist believes that the Pope hath Authority to dispense with the Laws of God, and absolve any one from the Obligation of keeping the Commandments. On the other side, the *Representer* affirms, *That the Pope has no Authority to dispense with the Law of God, and that there's no power upon Earth can absolve any one from the Obligation of keeping the Commandments:* This matter is not to be determined by the ones affirming, and the others denying: but by finding out, if possible, the true sense of the Church of *Rome* about this matter. And there are Three Opinions about it.

De Concess. Præbend. è proposuit. Abb. c. proposuit de Conc. Præbend. C. 15 Q 6. c. Auctoritate

1. Of those who assert, *That the Pope hath a power of dispensing in any Divine Law, except the Articles of Faith.* The Gloss upon the Canon Law saith, That where the Text seems to imply, that the Pope cannot dispense against the Apostle, it is to be understood of Articles of Faith. And *Panormitan* saith, This Exposition pleases him well; for the Pope may dispense in all other things: *contra Apostolum dispensat,* saith the Gloss on the Decree: And the *Roman* Editors in the Margin, refer to 34 *Dist. c. Lector* to prove it: And there indeed the Gloss is very plain in the case, *sic ergo Papa dispensat contra Apostolum:* And the *Roman* Correcters there justifie it, and say it is no absurd Doctrine as to positive Institutions, but the former *notable Gloss,* as *Panormitan* calls it, sets down the particulars wherein the Pope may dispense. As 1. Against the Apostles and their Canons. 2. Against

Sum. Angelic. v. dispensatio.

gainſt the Old Teſtament.   3. In Vows   4. In Oaths.   The *Summa Angelica* ſaith, the Pope may diſpenſe as to all the Precepts of the Old Teſtament.   And *Clavaſius* founds this Power upon the plenitude of the Popes Power, according to that Expreſſion in the Decretal mentioned, that he can, *ex plenitudine Poteſtatis de Jure ſupra Jus diſpenſare*; and without ſuch a Power, he ſaith, God would not have taken that care of his Church, which was to be expected from his Wiſdom. *Jacobatius* brings ſeveral inſtances of this Power in the Pope, and refers to the *Speculator* for more. *Jac. Almain* ſaith, That all the Canoniſts are of Opinion, that the Pope may diſpenſe againſt the Apoſtle; and many of their Divines, but not all: For, Jacobat. de Conciliis l. 5. p. 215. Almain. de poteſt Eccleſiæ, c. 13.

2. Some of their Divines held *that the Pope could not diſpenſe with the Law of God,* as that implies a proper *relaxation* of the *Law,* but could only *Authoritatively declare* that the Law did not oblige in ſuch a particular caſe; becauſe an Inferior could not take away the force of a Superiors Law; and otherwiſe there would be no fixed and immutable Rule in the Church; and if the Pope might diſpenſe in one Law of God, he might diſpenſe in the reſt. And of this Opinion were ſome of the moſt eminent School-Divines, as *Thomas Aquinas, Bonaventure, Major, Soto,* and *Catharinus,* who at large debates this Queſtion, and denies that the Pope hath any Power to diſpenſe with Gods Law: But then he adds, that the Pope hath a kind of *Prophetical Power* to *declare* in what Caſes the Law doth oblige, and in what not; which he parallels with the power of *declaring* the *Canon of Scripture*; and this he doth not by his own Authority, but by Gods; He confeſſeth the Pope cannot diſpenſe with thoſe precepts which are of themſelves indiſpenſable; nor alter the Sacraments; but then, ſaith he, there are ſome Divine Laws, which have a general force, but in particular caſes may be diſpenſed with; and in theſe caſes the Law is to be relaxed, ſo that the Relaxation ſeems to come from God himſelf: But he confeſſes this power is not to be often made uſe of; ſo that he makes this power to be no Act of Juriſdiction, but of *Prophetical Interpretation,* as he calls it; and he brings the Inſtance of *Caiaphas* to this purpoſe: And he adds, that the difference between the Divines and *Canoniſts* was but in Terms; for the *Canoniſts* were in the right as to the power, and the Divines in the manner of explaining it. Catharin. c. Cajetan. 6. p. 524

K   3. Others

3. Others have thought this too loose a way of explaining the Popes power and therefore they say, *That the Pope hath not a bare declaratory Power, but a real Power of dispensing in a proper sense in particular Cases*: For say they, the other is no act of Jurisdiction, but of Discretion, and may belong to other men as well as to the Pope; but this they look on as more agreeable to the Popes Authority and Commission; and a bare declaratory power would not be sufficient for the Churches Necessity; as *Sanchez* shews at large, and quotes many Authors for this Opinion; and *Sayr* more; and he saith *the Practice of the Church cannot be justified without it*. Which *Suarez* much insists upon; and without it, he saith, *the Church hath fallen into intolerable Errors*; and *it is evident*, he saith, *the Church hath granted real Dispensations, and not meer Declarations*. And he founds it upon Christs promise to *Peter*, *To thee will I give the Keys*, and the charge to him, *Feed my sheep*. But then he explains this Opinion, by saying that it is no formal Dispensation with the Law of God, but the matter of the Law is changed or taken away.

<small>Sanchez. de Matrim. l. 8. Dis. 6 n. 5. Sayr. Clavis Reg. l.6. c.11. Suarez.de vot. l. 6. c. 9. n. 7, 8, 9, 17.</small>

Thus I have briefly laid together the different Opinions in the Church of *Rome* about this power of dispensing with the Law of God, from which it appears, that they do all consent in the thing, but differ only in the manner of explaining it.

And I am therefore afraid our *Representer* is a very unstudied Divine, and doth not well understand their own Doctrine, or he would never have talked so boldly and unskilfully in this matter.

As to what he pretends, that *their Church teaches that every Lye is a Sin*, &c. it doth not reach the case; For the Question is not, Whether their Church teach men to lye, but, Whether there be not such a power in the Church, as by altering the Nature of things, may not make that not to be a Lye, which otherwise would be one: As their Church teaches that Men ought not to break their Vows; yet no one among them questions, but the Pope may dissolve the Obligation of a Vow, altho it be made to God himself. Let him shew then, how the Pope comes to have a power to release a Vow made to God, and not to have a power to release the Obligation to veracity among men.

Again,

Again, We do not charge them with delivering any such Doctrine, *That men may have Dispensations to lye and forswear themselves at pleasure*; for we know this Dispensing power is to be kept up as a great Mystery, and not to be made use of, but upon weighty and urgent causes, of great consequence and benefit to the Church, as their Doctors declare. But as to all matters of fact, which he alludes to, I have nothing to say to them; for our debate is only, whether there be such a power of Dispensation allowed in the Church of *Rome*, or not?

P. 45.

XX. *Of the Deposing Power.*

TO bring this matter into as narrow a compass as may be, I shall first take notice of his Concessions, which will save us a labour of proofs.

1. He yields *that the Deposing and King-killing power hath been maintained by some Canonists and Divines of his Church, and that it is in their opinion lawful, and annexed to the Papal Chair.*

P. 46.

2. *That some Popes have endeavoured to act according to this Power.*

But then he denies *that this Doctrine appertains to the Faith of his Church, and is to be believed by all of that Communion.* And more than that, he saith, *The affirming of it is a malicious calumny, a down-right falsity.*

Let us now calmly debate the matter, Whether according to the received principles of the Church of *Rome*, this be only a particular opinion of some Popes and Divines, or be to be received as a matter of Faith. The Question is not,

Whether those who deny it do account it an Article of Faith; for we know they do not: But whether upon the principles of the Church of *Rome* they are not bound to do it.

I shall only, to avoid cavilling, proceed upon the principles owned by our Author himself, *viz.*

1. *That the sense of Scripture, as understood by the community of Christians in all Ages since the Apostles, is to be taken from the present Church.*

P. 29

2. *That by the present Church he understands the Pastors and Prelates assembled in Councils, who are appointed by Christ and his Apostles*

P. 34.

files for the decision of controversies; and that they have infallible assistance.

P. 40, 41.   3. *That the Pope as the Head of the Church, hath a particular Assistance promised him, with a special regard to his Office and Function.*

If therefore it appear that Popes and Councils have declared this Deposing Doctrine, and they have received other things as Articles of Faith upon the same Declarations, Why should they then stick at yielding this to be an Article of Faith, as well as the other?

It is not denied, that I can find, that Popes and Councils for several ages have asserted and exercised the deposing power; but it is alledged against these Decrees and Acts. 1. That they were not grounded upon Universal Tradition. 2. That they had not Universal Reception.

Now, if these be sufficient to overthrow the Definitions of Councils, let us consider the consequences of it.

1. Then every man is left to examine the Decrees of Councils, whether they are to be embraced or not; for he is to judg whether they are founded on Universal Tradition; and so he is not to take the sense of the present Church for his Guide, but the Universal Church from Christs time: which overthrows a Fundamental principle of the *Roman* Church.

2. Then he must reject the pretended Infallibility in the Guides of the Church, if they could so notoriously err in a matter of so great consequence to the peace of Christendom as this was; and consequently their authority could not be sufficient to declare any Articles of Faith; and so all persons must be left at liberty to believe as they see cause, notwithstanding the Definitions made by Popes and Councils.

3. Then he must believe the Guides of the *Roman* Church to have been mistaken, not once or twice, but to have persisted in it for Five hundred years: which must take away, not only infallibility, but any kind of Reverence to the authority of it. For whatever may be said as to those who have depended on Princes, or favour their parties against the Guides of the Church, it cannot be denied that for so long time the leading party in that Church did assert and maintain the Deposing power; and therefore *Lessius* truly understood this matter, when he said, *That there*

there was scarce any Article of the Christian Faith, the denial whereof was more dangerous to the Church, or did precipitate Men more into Heresie and Hatred of the Church, than this of the Deposing Power; for, he says, *they could not maintain their Churches Authority without it.*

Discussio Decreti Magni Concil. Lateran. p. 89.

And he reckons up these ill Consequences of denying it.

P. 90, &c.

1. That the *Roman* Church hath erred for at least five hundred years, in a matter fundamental as to Government, and of great Moment: Which is worse than an Error about Sacraments, as Penance, Extream Unction, &c. and yet those who deny the Church can err in one, hold that it hath erred in a greater matter.

2. That it hath not only erred, but voluntarily and out of Ambition, perverting, out of Design, the Doctrine of the Primitive Church and Fathers concerning the Power of the Church, and bringing in another contrary to it, against the Right and Authority of Princes; which were a grievous sin.

3. That it made knowingly, unrighteous Decrees, to draw persons from their Allegiance to Princes; and so they became the causes of many Seditions and Rebellions, and all the ill consequences of them, under a shew of Piety and Religion.

4. That the Churches Decrees, Commands, Judgments and Censures may be safely contemned as Null, and containing intolerable Errors. And that it may require such things which good Subjects are bound to disobey.

5. That *Gregory* VII. in the Canon *Nos Sanctorum, &c. Urban* II. *Gregory* IX. the Councils of *Lateran* under *Alex* III. and *Innocent* III. the Councils of *Lyons*, of *Vienna*, of *Constance*, of *Lateran* under *Leo* X. and of *Trent*, have all grievously and enormously erred about this matter; For that it was the Doctrine of them all, he shews at large; and so Seven General Councils lose their Infallibility at one blow.

6. That the Gates of Hell have prevailed against the Church: For the true Church could never teach such pernicious Doctrine as this must be, if it be not true. And if it erred in this, it might as well err in any other Doctrine, and so Men are not bound to believe or obey it.

7. That Princes and all Laymen have just Cause to withdraw from their Church; because it shewed it self to be governed by a spirit of Ambition, and not by the Spirit of God; and not only

ly

[74]

ly fo, but they may juftly profecute all that maintain a Doctrine fo pernicious to Government, if it be not true.

Let us now fee what our Author faith to clear this from being a Doctrine of the Church of *Rome*.

1. *That for the few Authors that are abettors of this Doctrine, there are of his Communion Three times the number that publickly difown all fuch Authority.*

If this be true, it is not much for the Reputation of their Church, That there fhould be fuch a number of thofe who are liable to all thefe dreadful confequences, which *Leſſius* urges upon the deniers of it: But is it poffible to believe, there fhould be fo few followers of fo many Popes, and Seven General Councils, owned for fuch by the difowners of this Doctrine, except the *Lateran* under *Leo* 10? The poor *Eaftern* Chriftians are condemned for *Hereticks* by the Church of *Rome*, for refufing to fubmit to the Decrees of one General Council, either that of *Ephefus*, or of *Chalcedon* : and they plead for themfelves, That there was a mifinterpretation of their meaning, or not right underftanding one another about the difference of *Nature* and *Perfon*, which occafioned thofe Decrees. I would fain know, whether thofe Churches which do not embrace the Decrees of thofe Councils, are in a ftate of Herefie or not? If they be, then what muft we think of fuch who reject the Decrees of Seven General Councils, one after another, and give far lefs probable accounts of the Proceedings of thofe Councils in their Definitions, than the other do.

2. He faith, *Thofe who have condemned it, have not been in the leaft fufpected of their Religion, or of denying any Article of Faith.* Let any one judg of this by *Leſſius* his Confequences: And the Author of the firft Treatife againft the Oath of Allegiance faith in plain Terms, *That the Opinion that the Pope hath no fuch Power, is erroneous in Faith, as well as temerarious and impious*; And he proves it by this fubftantial argument; Becaufe they who hold it, muft fuppofe that the Church hath been for fometime in a damnable Error of Belief, and Sin of Practice: And he not only proves that it was defined by Popes and Councils, but for a long time univerfally received; and that no one Author can be produced before *Calvins* time, that denied this Power abfolutely, or in any cafe whatfoever. *But a few Authors that are Abettors*

of

Difcuff. Difcuff. Part 3. Sect 3. p. 1.

Philip. a SS. Trinit. Itiner. Orient l 5. c. 5. Clem. Galan. Concil. Eccl. Arm. Qu. 2. SS. 3 p 92.

Jefuits Loyalty, firft Treatife, p. 1, &c.

of it, faith our *Representer*: *Not one total Dissenter for a long time*, faith the other: And which of these is the true Representer? *The deniers of it not in the least suspected of their Religion*, faith one: *Their Opinion is erroneous in Faith, temerarious and impious*, faith the other. And a Professor of *Lovain*, now living, hath undertaken to shew, that the number is far greater of those who assert this Doctrine, than of those who deny it.

3. *If we charge their Church with this Opinion, may not they as well charge ours with the like; since Propositions as dangerous were condemned at* Oxford, July 26. 1683. *as held not by* Jesuits, *but by some among our selves?* This is the force of his Reasoning: But we must desire the Reader to consider the great disparity of the case. We cannot deny, that there have been men of ill Minds, and disloyal Principles, Factious and Disobedient, Enemies to the Government, both in Church and State; but have these Men ever had that countenance from the Doctrines of the Guides of our Church, which the Deposing Doctrine hath had in the Church of *Rome*? To make the case parallel, he must suppose our Houses of Convocation to have several times declared these Damnable Doctrines, and given Encouragement to Rebels to proceed against their Kings, and the University of *Oxford* to have condemned them; for this is truly the case in the Church of *Rome*; the Popes and Councils have owned, and approved, and acted by the Deposing Principle: but the Universities of *France*, of late years, have condemned it. How come the Principles of the Regicides among us to be parallel'd with this Doctrine, when the Principles of our Church are so directly contrary to them; and our Houses of Convocation would as readily condemn any such damnable Doctrines, as the University of *Oxford*? And all the World knows how repugnant such Principles are to those of the Church of *England*, and none can be Rebels to their Prince, but they must be false to our Church.

As to the personal Loyalty of many persons in that Church, as I have no Reason to question it, so it is not proper for me to debate it, if I did: since our business is not concerning Persons, but Doctrines; and it was of old observed concerning the *Epicureans*, That tho their principles did overthrow any true Friendship, yet many of them made excellent Friends.

P. 47. 48.
Auctoritas sedis apostolicæ vindicata adversus Natal. Alexand per Francisc. D. Enghien. Colon. A.D. 1684.

XXI. *Of Communion in One Kind.*

FOR our better proceeding in this Controverſie, I ſhall ſet down the State of it as clearly as I can.

1. The Queſtion is not, Whether the firſt Inſtitution of the Sacrament of the Euchariſt by Jeſus Chriſt, were in one Kind, or two: for all confeſs it was under both Kinds.

2. It is not, Whether both Kinds are not ſtill neceſſary for the due Celebration of it; for it is granted that both Kinds are neceſſary to be upon the Altar, or elſe there could be no compleat Sacrifice.

3. It is not, Whether the people may be wholly excluded from both Kinds, and ſo the Sacrifice only remain: for they grant that the people are bound to communicate in one Kind.

4. It is not concerning any peculiar and extraordinary Caſes, where no Wine is to be had, or there be a particular Averſion to it, or any ſuch thing, where poſitive Inſtitutions may be reaſonably preſumed to have no force: But concerning the publick and ſolemn Celebration, and participation of it in the Chriſtian Church.

5. It is not concerning the meer difuſe or neglect of it, But concerning the lawfulneſs of Excluding the people from both Kinds, by the Churches prohibition, notwithſtanding the Inſtitution of it by Chriſt in both Kinds, with a command to keep up the celebration of it to his ſecond coming.

Here now conſiſts the point in Controverſie, Whether the Church being obliged to keep up the Inſtitution in both Kinds, be not equally obliged to diſtribute both as our Saviour did, to as many as partake of it? Our Author not denying the Inſtitution, or the continuance of it, ſaith, *Our Saviour left it indifferent to receive it in one Kind, or both.* And that is the point to be examined.

1. He ſaith, *Chriſt delivered it to his Apoſtles, who only were then preſent, and whom he made Prieſts juſt before: yet he gave no command that it ſhould be ſo received by all the Faithful.*

But were not the Apoſtles all the Faithful then preſent? I pray in what capacity did they then receive it? As Prieſts? How

How did they receive the Bread before the *hoc facite*? As Priests or as faithful? It is ridiculous to suppose the *hoc facite* changed their capacity; and if it did, it only relates to consecrating, and not to receiving: but if Christ gave it only to the Apostles as Priests, then for all that I can see, the People are not at all concerned in one kind or other; but it was intended only for Priests: If the people be concerned, how came they to be so? Where is there any command but what refers to the first Institution? And it had been more plausible, according to this Answer, to exclude the People wholly, than to admit them to one Kind, and to debar them the other.

2. *Christ attributes the obtaining Life Everlasting, the end of the Institution, sometimes to receiving under both Kinds, sometimes under one,* John 6. 51, 57, 58. He could not easily have thought of any thing more against himself; for our Saviour there makes it as necessary to drink his Blood, as to eat his Flesh, *Verily, verily, I say unto you, Except you eat the Flesh of the Son of man, and drink his Blood, ye have no Life in you:* If this be understood of the Sacrament, as he saith, How is it possible for him to make the Cup indifferent? Unless it be indifferent whether the People be saved or not. [St. John 6. 51.]

3. *Christ himself administred the Sacrament to some of his Disciples under one kind only,* Luke 24. 30. But is he sure Christ did then administer the Sacrament to them? Or that if he did, the Cup was not implied, since breaking of Bread, when taken for an ordinary Meal in Scripture, doth not exclude drinking at it? But S. Augustin, he saith, (l. 49. *de Consensu Evangel.*) understands that place of the Sacrament. If he doth, it cannot be where he saith; for S. *Augustin* wrote but Four Books of that Subject: but l. 3. 25. he doth say something towards it; yet S. *Augustin* in another place supposes that these Disciples did both eat and drink. *The Disciples did not know him, but in the breaking of Bread; and truely he that doth not eat and drink Judgment to himself, doth in the breaking of Bread own Christ.* Where it is plain, that he applies both, to the breaking of Bread here spoken of. [Tract 2. in Epist. S. Joh.]

4. He saith, *it was the Custom of the Primitive Christians to give it under one kind to Children, the Sick, and to Men in a journey.* I would he had produced his Authorities to prove these things: for I can bring several to prove the direct contrary as to Chil-

dren, and sick Persons, and Travellers, and not only Ancient Writers, but the most Learned of their own Church. And therefore I cannot but wonder to find him saying, *This was attested by all Ancient Writers and Modern Historians.* But I have ever found those have been most mistaken, who produce *all Writers and Historians*, when it may be, there is not one that speaks home to the business. At least, we have here none mentioned, and therefore none to examin; and it would be too hard a task to search *All*.

5. He adds to this extravagancy, in saying, *That Receiving in one or both kinds, was indifferent for the first Four Hundred Years*; when the contrary is so manifest, that the most ingenious of their own Writers confess it. If any Persons did carry home one kind (which is very questionable, for *Baronius* and *Albaspinæus* say, they carried both Kinds) to receive it in times of Persecution, at what season they thought fit afterwards; This ought not to be set up against the general and constant Rule of the Church; which is attested, not only by *Cassander* and such like, but even by *Salmero*, *Ruardus Tapperus*, and *Lindanus*, who make no scruple of saying, The publick Celebration in the Primitive Church was in both Kinds. But then, how is it possible for us to judg better, what they thought themselves bound to do, than what they constantly observed in all their publick Celebrations? The Church is not accountable for the particular Fancies or Superstitions of Men; but what was observed in all publick Offices, we have reason to think the Church thought it self obliged so to do, out of regard to the Institution of Christ. And to shew how Universal this Observation was in the Church, those who give account of the *Eastern* Church say, That the *Greeks*, *Nestorians*, *Armenians*, *Maronites*, *Cophtites* and *Abyssins* do all observe it still, *viz.* That the publick Communicants do partake of both kinds. And not one of all these Churches, but think themselves bound to observe it, out of regard to the Institution of Christ; and why then should any think the Primitive Church thought it indifferent?

<small>Cotovic Itiner Hierosolymit. l. 2. c. 6. Histoir. Critique, p. 14.</small>

6. *The first Precept of receiving under both Kinds, was given to the Faithful by Pope* Leo, A. D. 443. *and confirmed by* Gelasius, A. D. 490. This is a great mistake, for *Leo* gave no Precept about it; but only told the People how they might certainly discover the *Manichees*, for they would conform in other things, but

but they would not taste of the Wine: which argued, that all other Communicants did then partake in both Kinds. *Gelasius* not only confirms the custom then used, but he saith, *That it is Scriledg to divide that Holy Mystery.* And surely he did not account Sacriledg an Indifferent thing.

7. Lastly he saith, *That those who receive in one Kind, are truely partakers of the whole Sacrament.* This is a new way of Concomitancy; we used to hear of *Whole Christ* under either Species, and that *Whole Christ* was therefore received: But how comes it to be *the whole Sacrament*, which consists of two distinct Parts? And if it be a Sacrifice, the Blood must be separated from the Body, else the Blood of Christ is not considered as shed, and so the Notion of the Sacrifice will be lost: Which is our next Head.

P. 52.

XXII. Of the MASS.

Under this Head, which is thought of so great Consequence in the *Roman* Church, I expected a fuller Representation than I here find; as about the *Opus Operatum*, i.e. how far the meer Act is effectual: About their *Solitary Masses*, when no Person receives but the Priest: About the People having so little to do, or understand, in all the other parts of the *Mass*: About the Rites and Ceremonies of the *Mass*, how useful and important they are: About reconciling the present Canon of the *Mass* with the present Practises: About offering up *Masses* for the honour of Saints. All which we find in the Council of *Trent*, but are omitted by our *Representer*; Who speaks of the *Mass*, as tho there were no controversy about it, but only concerning the Sacrifice there supposed to be offered up, and which he is far from true Representing: For the Council of *Trent* not only affirms *a true proper propitiatory Sacrifice to be there offered up for the quick and dead*, but denounces *Anathema*'s against those that deny it. So that the Question is not, Whether the Eucharist may not in the sense of Antiquity be allowed to be *a Commemorative Sacrifice*, as it takes in the whole Action: but whether in the *Mass* there be such a Representation made to God of *Christ's Sacrifice*, as to be it self a true and Propitiatory Sacrifice for the sins of the Quick and the Dead?

Sess. 22. cap. 2. can. 1, 2, 3, &c.

Now,

Now, all that our *Representer* faith to the purpose, is,

P. 53.   1. *That Christ bequeathed his Body and Blood at his last Supper, under the Species of Bread and Wine, not only a Sacrament, but also a Sacrifice.* I had thought it had been more proper to have offered a Sacrifice, than to have bequeathed it. And this ought to have been proved, as the foundation of this Sacrifice, *viz.* That Christ did at his last Supper offer up his Body and Blood as a Propitiatory Sacrifice to God. And then what need his suffering on the Cross?

2. *He gave this in charge to his Apostles, as the first and chief Priests of the New-Testament, and to their Successors, to offer.* But Where? When? and How? For we read nothing at all of it in Scripture. *Christ indeed did bid them do the same thing he had there done in his last Supper.* But did he then offer up himself, or not? If not, how can the Sacrifice be drawn from his action? If he did, it is impossible to prove the necessity of his dying afterwards.

3. *This Sacrifice was never questioned till of late years.* We say, it was never determined to be a *Propitiatory Sacrifice*, till of late. We do not deny the Fathers interpreting *Mal.* 1. 11. of an Offering under the Gospel; but they generally understand it of Spiritual and Eucharistical Sacrifices: and altho some of them, by way of accommodation, do apply it to the Eucharist, yet not one of them doth make it a *Propitiatory Sacrifice*, which was the thing to be proved: For, we have no mind to dispute about Metaphorical Sacrifices when the Council of *Trent* so positively decrees it to be a *True, Proper, and Propitiatory Sacrifice.*

XXIII. *Of PURGATORY.*

Here our Author begins with proving from Scripture and Antiquity, and then undertakes to explain the Doctrine of *Purgatory* from substantial Reasons.

1. As to his Proof from Scripture.

1. Is that from 2 *Maccab.* c. 12. where he faith, *Money was sent to Jerusalem, that Sacrifices might be offered for the slain:* and 'tis *recommended as a Holy Cogitation, to pray for the dead.*

To this, which is the main foundation of *Purgatory*, I answer, 1. It can never prove such a *Purgatory* as our Author asserts; For he supposes *a Sinner reconciled to God, as to eternal punishment*, before he be capable of *Purgatory*; but here can be no such supposition; for these men died in the sin of *Achan*, which was not known till their bodies were found among the slain. Here was no Confession, or any sign of Repentance, and therefore if it proves any thing, it is *deliverance from eternal punishment*, and for such as dye in their sins without any shew of Repentance. 2. We must distinguish the Fact of *Judas* from the interpretation of *Jason*, or his Epitomizer. The Fact of *Judas* was according to the strictness of the Law, which required in such cases a *Sin Offering*; and that is all which the *Greek* implies. Απέστειλεν εἰς Ἱεροσόλυμα προσαγαγεῖν περὶ ἁμαρτίας θυσίαν. And so *Leo Allatius* confesses all the best *Greek* Copies agree, and he reckons Twelve of them. Now what doth this imply, but that *Judas* remembring the severe punishment of this sin in the case of *Achan*, upon the people, sent a Sin-offering to *Jerusalem*? But saith *Leo Allatius*, *It was the sin of those men that were slain*. I grant it. But the Question is, Whether the *Sin-offering* respected the dead or the living? For the Law in such a case required *a Sin-offering for the Congregation*. And why should not we believe so punctual a Man for the Law, as *Judas*, did strictly observe it in this point? *But the Author of the Book of* Maccabees *understands it of those that were slain*. I do not deny it: but then 3. We have no Reason to rely upon his Authority in this matter; which I shall make appear by a parallel instance. He doth undoubtedly commend the fact of *Razias* in *Killing himself* (2 Macc. 14. 42) when he saith he did it, 'Ευγενῶς, *like a brave Man*; and if he had thought it a fault in him, he would never have given such a Character of it, but he would have added something of caution after it. And it is no great advantage to *Purgatory*, for him that commends Self-murder, to have introduced it. The most probable account I can give of it is, That the *Alexandrian Jews*, of whose number, *Jason of Cyrene* seems to have been, had taken in several of the Philosophical Opinions, especially the *Platonists*, into their Religion, as appears by *Philo*; and *Bellarmin* himself confesses, that *Plato* held a *Purgatory*: and they were ready to apply

P. 57.

Leo Allat. de Purgat. p. 889.

Levit 4. 13.

Bellar de Purgat. l. 1. c. 2:

ply what related to the Law, to their Platonick Notions. So here the Law appointed a Sin-offering with respect to the Living; but *Jalon* would needs have this refer to the dead: and then sets down his own remarks upon it, That *it was a holy cogitation to pray for the dead*, as our Author renders it. If it were *holy* with respect to the Law, there must be some ground for it in the Law: and that we appeal to, and do not think any particular Fancies sufficient to introduce such a Novelty as this was, which had no Foundation either in the Law or the Prophets. And it would be strange for a new Doctrine to be set up, when the Spirit of Prophecy was ceased among them.

P. 55.

But S. August. *held these Books for Canonical*, and saith, *they are so received by the Church*, l. 18. de Civit. Dei. To answer this, it is sufficient to observe, not only the different opinions of others before mentioned as to these Books: But that as *Canus*

Can. l. 2. c. 10. ad 4.

notes, *it was then lawful to doubt of their Authority*: And he goes as low as *Gregory* I. Whom he denies not to have rejected them. And I hope we may set the authority of one against the

Aug. cont. 2d Epist. Gaudent l. 2. c. 23.

other; especially when St. *Augustin* himself, being pressed hard with the fact of *Razias*, confesses, 1. *That the Jews have not the Book of* Maccabees *in their Canon, as they have the Law, the Prophets, and the Psalms, to whom our Lord gave Testimony as to his Witnesses*. Which is an evident proof, he thought not these Books sufficient to ground a Doctrine upon, which was not found in the other. 2. *That however this Book was not unprofitably received by the Church, if it be soberly read and heard.* Which implies a greater caution than St. *Augustin* would ever have given, concerning a Book he believed truly Canonical:

De purgat. l. 1. c. 3.

But saith *Bellarmin*, *his meaning is only to keep men from imitating the Example of Razias*: whereas that which they pressed S. *Augustin* with, was not merely the Fact, but the *Character* that is given of it. *Sanctarum Scripturarum Auctoritate laudatus est Razias*, are their very Words in S. *Augustin*: and therefore the Caution relates to the Books, and not merely to his Example: and he lessens the Character given by the Author, when he saith, *He chose to dye nobly*; *It had been better*, saith he, *to have died humbly*. But the other is the *Elogium* given in the Heathen Histories, and better becomes brave Heathens, than true Martyrs. Can any one now think S. *Augustin* believed this Writer Divinely ly inspired, or his Doctrine sufficient to ground a point of Faith upon ? And I wonder they should not every jot as well commend *Self-murder* as an *Heroical Act*, as prove the Doctrine of Purgatory from these words of *Jason*, or his Epitomizer. For the argument from the authority of the Book, will hold as strongly for one as the other. And yet this is the *Achilles* for Purgatory, which *Natalis Alexander* (whom our Author follows in this matter) saith, *is a Demonstrative Place against those that deny it*. But I must proceed.

Natal. Alex. Sec. 4 Diff 4.

2. *Purgatory is plainly intimated by our Saviour*, Matt. 12. 32. *Whosoever speaketh against the Holy-Ghost, it shall not be forgiven him, neither in this world, neither in the world to come.* By which words, Christ evidently supposes, that some sins are forgiven in the world to come. I am so far from discerning this plain intimation, that I wonder how any came to think of it out of this place. Well, *But doth it not hence follow, that sins may be forgiven in the world to come?* Not near so plainly, as that Sins will not be forgiven in the World to come. *Not that particular sin, but others may*: How doth that appear ? What intimation is there, that any Sins not forgiven here, shall be forgiven there ? Or that any Sins here remitted as to the Eternal Punishment, shall be there remitted as to the Temporal ? and without such a kind of Remission, nothing can be inferred from hence. *But if there be a Remission in another World, it can be neither in Heaven nor Hell, therefore it must be in Purgatory*. But those who own a Remission of Sins in another World, say it will be on the Day of Judgment : For the actual deliverance of the Just from punishment, may be not improperly called the full Remission of their Sins. So S. *Augustin*, whom he quotes plainly saith, *Si nulla remitterentur in judicio illo novissimo, &c.* c. *Julian*, l. 6. c. 5. where it is evident S. *Augustin* takes this place to relate to the Day of Judgment; and so in the other, (*De Civit. Dei* l. 21. c. 24.) But as he supposed a Remission, so he did a purgation as by Fire in that day. *In illo judicio pœnas quasdam purgatorias futuras*. *De Civit. Dei* l. 20. c. 25. And so he is to be understood on *Psal.* 37. to which he applies 1 *Cor.* 3. 15. But our Author was very much out, when he saith S. *Augustin* applied 1 *Pet.* 3. 15. to some place of temporal chastisement in another World, when *Bellarmin* sets himself to confute St. *Augustin* about it, as understanding it of this World. And therefore he

P. 56.

Bell. de An. Christi l. 4. c. 13.

he hath little caufe to boaft of St. *Auguftins* authority about *Purgatory*, unlefs he had brought fomething more to the purpofe out of him. His other Teftimonies of Antiquity are not worth confidering, which he borrows from *Natalis Alexander*: that of *Dionyfius Areopag. Eccl. Hierarch.* c 7. is a known Counterfeit, and Impertinent, relating to a Region of Reft and Happinefs: and fo do *Tertullians Oblations for the dead*, -*De Cor. Milit.* c. 3. For they were Euchariftical, as appears by the ancient Liturgies, being made for the greateft Saints. St. *Cyprian* Ep. 66. fpeaks of *an Oblation for the Dead*: and he there mentions the *Natilitia* of the Martyrs: but by comparing that with his *Epift.* 33. it will be found that he fpeaks of the *Anniverfary Commemoration of the Dead*, which fignifies nothing to Purgatory, for the beft men were put into it: and St. *Cyprian* threatens it as a punifhment to be left out of the *Dyptichs*: but furely it is none to efcape Purgatory: *Arnobius l.* 4. only fpeaks of *praying for the Dead*, which we deny not to have been then ufed in the Church, not with refpect to any temporary pains in *Purgatory*, but to the Day of Judgment: and therein lies the true ftate of the Controverfie, with refpect to antiquity; which is not, Whether any folemn prayers were not then made for the dead: But whether thofe prayers did relate to their deliverance out of a ftate of punifhment before the Day of Judgment. For whatever ftate Souls were then fuppofed to be in, before the great Day, if there could be no deliverance till the Day of Judgment, it fignifies nothing to the prefent Queftion.

As to the Vifion of *Perpetua* concerning her Brother *Dinocrates* who died at Seven Years old, being baptized, it is hardly reconcilable to their own Doctrine, to fuppofe fuch a Soul in Purgatory: I will not deny that *Perpetua* did think fhe faw him in a worfe condition, and thought likewife that by her Prayers fhe brought him into a better, for fhe faw him playing like little children, and then fhe awaked, and concluded that fhe had given him eafe: But is it indeed come to this, that fuch a Doctrine as Purgatory muft be built on fuch a Foundation as this? I do not call in queftion the Acts of *Perpetua*, nor her fincerity in relating her Dream; but muft the Church build her Doctrines upon the Dreams or Vifions of Young Ladies, tho very devout? for *Ubia Perpetua* was then but Twenty Two, as fhe faith her felf: but none are to be blamed, who make ufe of the beft fupports their Caufe will afford.

It

It is time now to see what strength of Reason he offers for Purgatory. 1. He saith; *When a sinner is reconciled to God, tho the Eternal punishment due to his sins is always remitted, yet there sometimes remains a temporal penalty to be undergone; as in the case of the* Israelites, *and* David. But doth it hence follow, that there is a temporal penalty that must be undergone either here or hereafter, without which there will be no need of *Purgatory*? Who denies, that God in this Life, for example sake, may punish those whose sins he hath promised to remit as to another World? This is therefore a very slender Foundation. 2. *There are some sins of their own nature light and venial.* I will not dispute that; but suppose there be, must men go then into Purgatory for mere Venial Sins? What a strange Doctrine doth this appear to any Mans Reason? That God should forgive the greater sins, and require so severe a punishment for sins in their own Nature venial, i. e. so inconsiderable in their Opinion, that no man is bound to confess them; which do not interrupt a state of Grace; which require only an implicite detestation of them; which do not deserve eternal punishment; which may be remitted by Holy Water, or a Bishops Blessing, as their Divines agree 3 *That to all sins some penalty is due to the Justice of God.* And what follows from hence but the necessity of Christs Satisfaction? but how doth it appear, that after the Expiation of Sin by Christ, and the remission of eternal punishment, there still remains a necessity of farther satisfaction for such a temporal penalty in another World? 4. *That generally speaking few men depart out of this Life, but either with the guilt of venial sins, or obnoxious to some temporal punishment*; No doubt all men are obnoxious by their sins to the punishment of another World; but that is not the point, but whether God hath declared, That altho he remits the eternal punishment, he will not the temporal; and altho he will forgive thousands of pounds, he will not the pence and farthings we owe to him: But if Mortal Sins be remitted as to the guilt, and Venial do not hinder a State of Grace, what room is there for vindictive Justice in *Purgatory.*

P. 57.

S Th. part 3. q. 87 art 3. in cor. v. Marsil. Column. Hydragio'og. Sect 7. c. 3. n. 32 Sect 3. c. 2. n. 15. 29. c. 3 n. 1. Bell. deCultuSanct. l. 3. c. 7. Sect. secundo.

Yet this is the Doctrine which so much weight is laid upon; that *Bellarmine* saith, *They must go directly to Hell, who do not believe Purgatory.* If this be true, why was it not put into the

DePurgatorio l. 1. c. 11. SS. Hæc. sunt.

Representation, that we might understand the danger of not believing so credible, so reasonable a Doctrine as this? But we believe it to be a much more dangerous thing to condemn others for not believing a Doctrine which hath so very slender a pretence either to Scripture or Reason.

XXIV. *Of Praying in an unknown Tongue.*

THE Question in short is, Whether the Church Service, at which persons are bound to assist, ought not to be in a Language understood by those who are bound to assist?

59. P. For our Author grants, *That a Papist is bound to assist at the Church-Service, and to hear* Mass; but he is not bound to understand the Words there spoken.

This is a plain state of the case; and one would have thought St. *Pauls* Discourse about Edification in the Church-Service, and a known Tongue, and the Primitive practice, had deserved a little consideration, but not a Word is said to either of them; and the whole is so managed, as tho there had been no Rule, or any appearance of practice to the contrary. But I must consider what he doth say,

1. *The Mass is a Sacrifice:* And what then? Have they no other Church Service but the Mass? What then becomes of their Breviaries, Litanies, and all other Offices? But suppose the Priests Office in the *Mass*, be to offer the Sacrifice; are there no Prayers in the Canon of the *Mass*, wherein the people are concerned? Why must not they understand what P. 61. they are required to assist in *Prayer* for? If they have *English* Books, as he saith, to teach them every part and Ceremony of the *Mass*, why not as well the Prayers in the *Mass*, wherein they are to join? They tell us, *It is unseasonable then for the People to say their Beads, and other Devotions:* And I suppose as unseasonable to talk, or think of other matters. Why then should not they know what it is they are to do, and what Petitions they are then to make to God? Are there no Responses to be made? No Lessons to be read? No Creed to be professed? Doth not the Priest speak to the People to pray, and they answer him? Is there no Thanksgiving after the Communion which the people is concerned,

cerned in? We are as much for *their Devout Affections*, as they can be; but we think they are not hindred by understanding what they are about: We cannot but wonder, that any man should say, *That it nothing concerns his Devotion, that the* Mass *is in* Latin, if he understand it not. Is it no part of Devotion to joyn in the publick prayers, not meerly by rote, but from a due apprehension of the matter contained in them? He requires, *That they accompany the Priest in Prayer and Spirit*: And why not in understanding also? *But the Church hath so ordered it:* And that is the thing we complain of, as done against St. *Paul*, against the Primitive Church, against the natural sense of Mankind, who think it is fit for them to know what they do, especially in the Worship of God: *But it is to preserve Unity:* Methinks however Unity in Spirit and Understanding is better than without it: *There are other good Reasons:* I know not one good one; and if there were more, he would have produced them: *The greatest part is said in a low voice, that it is not possible he should hear it:* And to what purpose should it be spoken louder, if they are not to understand it? But why so low in publick? Yet the people might have Books, and joyn, if they understood what was said. But why should not the rest be understood, which is spoken as if it were.

2. As to other Offices, he saith, *He is taught, that he may perform them in a Language which he understands not, with great benefit to his Soul, and the acceptance of God, if at those occasions he endeavours to raise his thoughts to Heaven, and fix his heart upon his Maker.* But the Question is not, Whether a Man may not have devout Thoughts at that time, but whether he can perform his part in the publick Offices, with true Devotion, without Understanding? For the publick Offices of Devotion were designed for the uniting the Hearts and Desires of the people in the same things. It is not, Whether one Man may not pray for Heaven and another for fair Weather, and another for pardon of his Sins, and a Fourth for Patience and so on, in the same place, and at the same time, for all this might be done as well in a *silent Meeting*, where not a Word is spoken. But there being one Form of Praying for all to join together in that with the united force of the whole Congregation, their Petitions may go up to Heaven; The Matter now in dispute is, Whether it be not necessary in order to this united De-

votion, that the people all know what they pray for? And one would think nothing need to be said to prove this: But what our Author adds in justification of this, overthrows all publick Devotion; For he saith, *It is not necessary to have attention on the Words, or on the Sense of Prayers, but rather purely on God:* Which is to make all publick Forms unnecessary, and to turn all Devotion into *Prayer* of *Contemplation:* For if this be true, all Forms whatsoever are not only useless, but burdensome; and by the stinting the Spirit, do hinder the nimbler flights of the Soul, in pure silence towards God: And this principle must lead men to *Enthusiasms*, and unintelligible Unions; and make them despise *Forms* as a mean and dull Dispensation.

But at last he saith, *A Petitioner may accompany his Petition with an earnest desire of obtaining it, tho the Language in which it is written, be unknown to him.* Very true, if he indited the matter of the Petition, and trusted another to put it into that Language, which the Person to whom he makes it, doth understand, but not his own: But all Languages are alike to Gods Infinite Wisdom, and so there can be no pretence on that account, to keep only to some particular Tongues, tho unknown to the Party; and if it were so to all men, no man would have a Petition presented in a Language which he did not know: But in prayer to God, the design of it is not to acquaint him with something which he knew not, but to excite the hearts and affections of men to an earnest desire of the things which are fit for them to ask: Now let any man undertake to prove, that mens affections are as easily moved by words they do not understand, as by those they do: and I will give up this Cause.

XXV. *Of the Second Commandment.*

THE Dispute about this, is not,
Whether the Second Commandment may be found in any of their Books, but by what Authority it comes to be left out in any: As he confesses it is *in their short Catechisms and Manuals:* but not only in these, for I have now before me the Reformed Office of the Blessed Virgin, Printed at *Salamanca*, A. D. 1588. published by Order of *Pius* V. where it is so left out: And so in the English Office at *Antwerp*, A. D. 1658. I wish he had told

told us in what publick Office of their Church it is to be found: but himself pleads for the leaving it out, when he saith, *The People are in no danger of Superstition or Idolatry by it; since the First Commandment secures them from it; and there is nothing in this, but what is vertually contained in the First, and is rather an Explanation, than a new and distinct Precept.* But is this so plain and clear, that a Mans Conscience can never make any just and reasonable Doubt concerning it? There is a terrible sanction after it; and men had need go upon very good Grounds in a matter of such moment. Hath God himself any where declared this to be only an Explication of the First Commandment? Have the Prophets, or Christ and his Apostles ever done it? How then can any mans Conscience be safe in this matter? For it is not a trifling Controversie, whether it be a distinct Commandment, or an Explication of the First; but the Lawfulness or Unlawfulness of the Worship of Images depends very much upon it: For if it be only an Explication of the First, then unless *one takes Images to be Gods*, their Worship is lawful, and so the Heathens were excused in it, who were not such Ideots: but if it be a new and distinct Precept, then the Worshipping any Image or Similitude, becomes a grievous sin, and exposes men to the Wrath of God in that severe manner mentioned in the end of it: And it is a great confirmation that this is the true meaning of it, because all the Primitive Writers of the Christian Church, not only thought it a sin against this Commandment, but insisted upon the force of it against those Heathens who denied that they took their Images for Gods: And therefore this is a very insufficient Account of leaving out the *Second Commandment.*

P. 64.

XXVI. *Of Mental Reservations.*

UNder this Head he denies Two Things.
1. *That they are ever taught to break Faith with Hereticks.*
2. *That their Church doth allow any Equivocations, or Mental Reservations.*

As to the former I am sincerely glad to find a Principle so destructive to all humane Society, so utterly disowned, when he saith, *He is taught to keep Faith with all sorts of People, of whatsoever*

P. 64.

ever judgment or perswasion they be; and to stand to his Word, and observe his Promise given, or made to any whatsoever. And whatever Opinions and Practices there may have been of that kind formerly, we hope there will never be occasion given to revive that dispute.

2. As to the Second, We embrace his Declaration against it, and hope there is no Equivocation, or Mental Reservation in it. But there are some things which must here be taken notice of.

1. We cannot deny that there are Authors in Communion with his Church, which may be charged with teaching another Doctrine; and those not a few, nor inconsiderable; who not only allow the Practice of Mental Reservations and Equivocations, but say with great confidence, it hath been received in the *Roman* Church for no less than Four hundred years; and that in some Cases they are all still agreed in it. See *Parsons* Treatise of *Mitigation, c. 7. Sect. 2. 3. c. 10 Sect. 1.*

2. We do not deny, that *Innocent* XI. hath condemned Equivocations, and Mental Reservations in Swearing, as *at least Scandalous and Pernicious in Practise*; and therefore we cannot charge the Pope with abetting this Doctrine. But we cannot but reflect on what our Author said about the Deposing Doctrine, *That although Popes had believed it, and acted by it, yet the greater number opposed it.* And what shall we say in this Case, if the Generality of their Casuists in some Cases approve it and think it no *Lie or Perjury*, as in that of *Confession*; but if it be really so in any one Case, then it may be some other fault; but it is not a *Lie or Perjury* in any other, when a Man doth not think himself bound to speak all he knows.

3. That as we highly commend the Popes condemning such Doctrines and Practises now; so we have Reason to think the contrary did not once want the encouragement and approbation of the *Roman* See. As may be found in the Resolution of some Cases by *Pius* V relating to some *Missionaries*, who were to be sent hither; and then it was declared, That if they were summon'd before our Judges, they might *Sophistice Jurare & Sophistice Respondere*; and that they were not bound to answer according to the Intention of the Judges, but according to some true sense of their own, *i. e.* which was made true by the help of

Apud G Abbot de Mendacio &c. in Præf p.6,&c.

of a Mental Refervation. But it is very well, that now the very fame things are condemned at *Rome*, as *fcandalous and pernicious in practice*.

XXVII. Of a Death-Bed Repentance.

WE have no difference with them about this matter, as far as they hold to thefe points: 1. *That men are ftrictly obliged to work out their Salvation with fear and trembling in time of Health.* 2. *That it is very dangerous to defer their Repentance to the laft.* 3. *That if any are furprized, they ought in charity to have all poffible affiftance, to put them into the beft way for their Salvation.*

But yet there may be fome particular Doctrines owned in the Church of *Rome*, which may give men too much encouragement to put off true Repentance; as 1. The eafinefs of being put into a ftate of Grace by the Sacrament of Penance; for which no more is required *than removing the impediment*; as appears by the Council of *Trent*. Seff. 7. Can. 6. and afterwards it defines *that bare Attrition doth fufficiently difpofe a Man to receive Grace in that Sacrament*, Seff. 14. c. 4. So that altho a Man hath led a very bad Life, if he hath but this *Attrition* for his fins when he doth confefs them, he is put into a ftate of Grace by this Sacrament. And what can any Man expect more, and what can he do lefs! I do not mean a bare *natural Attrition*, the fufficiency whereof is condemned by *Innocent* XI. in the fame Propofitions (Fifty feventh) but that which the Council of *Trent* calls *imperfect contrition, i. e.* a good Motion in a Mans mind to forfake his fins for fear of punifhment, if really no more be required for a ftate of Grace but this, it is no wonder if men put off the doing of that which may be done at any time fo eafily by the help of a Prieft.

2. The Treafure of the Church is another thing which is very apt to hinder Mens fpeedy Repentance; for by that they believe there is a ftock ready of fo many Merits and Satisfactions of others, if duely applied to them by Indulgences, that they need not be at fuch pains to *work out their own falvation with fear and trembling*. When a Man by the Sacrament of Penance is put into

into a state of Grace, the Eternal Punishment is discharged, and nothing remains but some Temporal pains: and to ease him of these he hath many helps but especially the Treasure of the Church, which the Pope hath the dispensing of, as he is bound to believe: and by Indulgences he may easily get off some Thousands of Years of Purgatory Pains; and if these should fail him, there is another help yet left, which is leaving a stock for Prayers for his Soul when he dies; *which, even our Author assures him, are very available towards his speedier release out of Purgatory*, p. 58.

XXVIII. Of FASTING.

THE Question here is, Whether a Man doth not observe their Churches Command about Fasting who forbears all forbidden things, but takes liberty in those which are not forbidden?

It is not, Whether they may not break the Commands of God, against *Gluttony* and *Drunkenness*: But whether they break the Law of the Church about Fasting? And notwithstanding what our Author hath said, I see no Reason for the Affirmative. I do not deny, 1. That it is a very indifferent sort of Fasting, *to abstain from Flesh, unless all other sorts of Excesses at the same time be carefully avoided*. 2. *That Excesses on such days are more scandalous, because there is a pretence of Fasting*. 3. That God's Command doth at all times forbid Intemperance. Which are the chief things he insists upon. But yet this doth not reach the point, which is about their *Churches Command*. For their Casuists distinguish Fasting into 1. *Natural*: which is total Abstinence: and this is required only in order to receive the Eucharist. 2. *Moral*: which is the same with Temperance, or Fasting for Health. 3. *Ecclesiastical*: which is defined by them to be, *An Abstinence from Food forbidden by the Church*. And if this Definition be true, it cannot be broken but by eating what the Church hath prohibited.

P. 69.

P. 71.

And therefore their Casuists, as far as I can find, are agreed in these things,

1. That

1. That a Man may eat a full Meal of what is not forbidden, and not break the Churches Precept of Fasting, provided Vespers be first said. And the later Casuists blame *Covarruvias* for making any scruple about it. *If a Mans Excess comes to be a Mortal sin; yet for all that,* saith *Reginaldus, He shall not be judged as a breaker of his Fast.* Nay, *Lessius* goes further, and saith, *He doth not lose the Merit of Fasting. Quamvis aliquis multum excedat non solvit Jejunium,* saith *Card. Tolet.* And *Paulus Zacchias* saith, *This is the common Opinion;* and he thinks the Intention of *the Church is sufficiently answered.* And so doth *Pasqualigus* in his *Praxis* of Fasting.

> Reginald. Praxis l. 4. e. 1 4. n. 163.
> Less. de Justit. l 4. c. 2. Dub. 2. n. 10
> Instruct. Sacred. l. 6. c. 2, n. 4.
> P. Zacch. Qu. Medico. legales l. 5. tit. 1. Qu. 1. p. 29, 30, 31.
> Pasqual. Decis. 120. n 5.
> Dian. Sam. v. Jejun. n. 7.
> Zach. Pasqualigi. Praxis Jejunii Eccles. Decis. 116, n. 3. Dec. 117. 1, 2, 3.

2. A Man may drink Wine, or other drink, as often as he pleaseth, without breaking his Fast. He may *toties quoties bibere,* saith *Diana. Zach. Pasqualigus,* who hath Written most fully on this Subject, shews, *That it is the general Opinion, that no quantity of Wine or other drink, tho taken without any Necessity, is a violation of the Precept of Fasting;* no, not although the Wine be taken for nourishment, because the Church doth not forbid it; but this last, he saith, *is not the general, but the more probable Opinion.*

3. A Man may eat something when he drinks, to prevent its doing him hurt; besides his good Meal, he may take what quantity he pleases of Sweet-meats or Fruit; he may have a good Refection at Night, and yet not break this strict Precept of Fasting; *For the eating as often as one drinks, it is the common Opinion,* saith the same Casuist (who was no *Jesuit*) *That it is not forbidden, because it is taken by way of a Medicine;* and he quotes a great number of their *Casuists* for it. *A Collation at evening is allowed,* saith he. And *Lessius* saith, *There is no certain Rule for the Quantity of it.* And *Card. Tolet* saith, *very large ones are allowed* at Rome *by the Popes Connivence; even in the Court of* Rome, saith *Reginaldus.* And now I leave the Reader to judge of the severity of Fasting required in the Church of Rome.

> Decis. 119. n. 2. Decis. 86. n. 34.
> Less. ubi supr. n. 11.
> Tolet. ubi sub.
> Regin ubi sup. n. 185.

XXIX. *Of Divisions and Schisms in the Church.*

TWO things he saith upon this Head.
1. *That they are all agreed in matters of Faith.*
2. *That they only differ in some School Points*; from whence he infers, That they have no Schisms or Separations among them.

But that this is no just consequence, will appear by the Schisms and Separations among us, made by such who profess to agree in all matters of Faith. Yet let us see how he proves that they agree in all matters of Faith; *because they agree to submit equally to the Determinations of the Church.*

Now this very way evidently proves that they do not all agree, because they do not equally submit to the Churches determinations. For,

1. Some say they are bound to submit to the Churches Determinations, as it represents the Universal Church; Others say no: but as the Churches Power is virtually lodged in the Guides of it. Now this is a very material Difference: For if it be on the former Account, then not the Popes and Councils Declarations are to be regarded, but as they express the sense of the Universal Church; and so the Majority of Votes, and Numbers in the Representative and Diffusive Church is chiefly to be regarded. And on this Ground some reject the Deposing Power, tho plainly decreed by Popes and Councils: but they unhinge their Churches Authority by it. Now how is it possible for them to agree about matters of Faith, who differ fundamentally about the way how any things come to be matters of Faith? If they be decreed by Popes and Councils, say some; and so the Deposing Power is become an Article of Faith. No such matter, say others, for a greater Number in the diffusive Church oppose it, as in the *Gallican* Church, and elsewhere. Very well! But how then can these Parties be said to agree in matters of Faith, and an equal Submission to the Determinations of the Church?

2. Some again say, That it is not the consent of the present Church can make any Article of Faith, but there must be an

Universal

Universal Tradition from the Apostles times. And so they tell us the Deposing Power can never be an Article of Faith, because it wants the Consent of all the Ages before *Gregory* VII. So that upon this Ground there can be no Article of Faith which cannot be proved to be thus delivered down to us. Others again say, this is in effect to give up their Cause, knowing the impossibility of proving particular Points in this manner: and therefore they say, the present Church is wholly to be trusted for the sense of the foregoing.

Now these differences are still on Foot in their Church; and from these do arise daily disputes about Matters of Faith, and the Seat of Infallibility, whether in the Guides, or the body of the Church: if the former, whether in the Church Representative, or Virtual? whether the Personal Infallibility of the Pope be a matter of Faith or not? Our Author saith, Not; others say yes: and yet he saith, *they are agreed in matters of Faith*: So that by his own Confession they differ about other things than mere School-points.

But suppose they were *agreed in Articles of Faith*, can there be no Schisms or Divisions in their Church? What thinks he of all the Schisms between Popes and Popes? Of all the Schisms between the Popes and the Emperors Parties? Which were as notorious, and scandalous, and mischievous, as ever were in the World. What thinks he of the Schisms between the Bishops and the Regular Orders, which were as cross and peevish towards the Bishops and Secular Clergy, as our Dissenters themselves? And among the Regular Orders, what Heats and Contentions have been, *Not about the Practice of a devout Life*, I assure him, but about matters of Doctrine: and which both Parties severally plead to be matters of Faith? As in the noted Controversies of this last Age, about the Immaculate Conception of the Blessed Virgin, the power of Grace, and the Popes Personal Infallibility: and they cannot say they are as yet agreed about these things.

XXX. *Of Friars and Nuns.*

OUR Dispute is not, About the lawfulness of retiring from the World by such Persons who are rendred unfit for doing Service in it; and the more they spend their time in Devotion and Contemplation, so much the better.

But it lies in these Things,

1. Whether the Perfection of a Christian State of Life lies in being cloystered up from the World, or labouring to do good in it? For this was the great snare made use of, to draw men into it, because they represented this as the most perfect state; whereas according to the Doctrine and Example of Christ and his Apostles, the active Life of doing good, is far beyond it.

2. Whether, altho such a retirement be allowed, it be a thing pleasing to God, to tye such Persons up by indispensable Vows, whatever their Circumstances may be, not to alter that State of Life; who either in Youth, or through Force, Passion, or Discontent, have entred into it? And this may be so much rather questioned, because those who assert the Pope may dispense, go upon this Ground, Because Circumstances may alter the Obligation of a Vow; and when a greater good is to be attained, it ceaseth to oblige; which to my apprehension doth not prove the Popes power to dispense, but the dispensible Nature of the Vows themselves.

3. Whether all things of this nature being liable in continuance of time, to great Degeneracy and Corruptions; and the numbers of such Places being unserviceable either to Church or State, it be not in the power of the King and States of the Kingdom, to dissolve and reduce them to ways more suitable to the Conveniences of both?

As to what he discourses about *Councils of Perfection, the Distractions of the World, the Corruptions of the best Things,* &c. They reach not the main points, but are only general Topicks, which we are not concerned to debate.

XXXI. *Of Wicked Principles and Practices.*

THE *Misrepresenter* charges the Church of *Rome* with many horrid Practices, as the *French* and *Irish* Massacres, the Murders of Two Kings of *France*, the Holy League, the Gun-powder-Treason, &c. And charges these as being done according to the Principles of that Church.

But in answer to this he saith, 1. In General, *That the Doctrine of it is holy, teaching the Love of God and our neighbour, and that none can be saved by Faith alone.* In which Doctrine we heartily concur with them. 2. *That altho many uncertain things pass for certain, and false for true, yet he cannot deny that all ranks and degrees of men have been corrupted among them, being scandalous in their Lives, wicked in their designs, without the Fear of God in their hearts, or care of their own Salvation.* This is a general acknowledgment, but no particular Answer to the things objected. 3. *That the whole Church is not to be charged for the sake of such villanies.* Very true, unless some Doctrine owned in that Church gave encouragement to them: As suppose any should ever have fallen into Rebellion upon the belief of the Deposing Power; is not that Doctrine chargeable with the Consequences of it? They are extremely to blame who charge a Church with what her Members do in direct Opposition to her Doctrine; but it is quite another Case, when the main Ground we alledge for their Actions is some allowed Principle in it. 4. *They are not accountable for the Actions of every Bishop, Cardinal, or Pope; for they extend not their Faith beyond the Declaration of General Councils.* But suppose General Councils have declared such Doctrines, and Popes act but according to them; is not their Church then accountable for their Actions? 5. *There is more Praying and Fasting, and receiving the Sacraments, more visiting the Prisoners, and the Sick, more Alms-giving in any of our neighbouring Popish Towns, as* Paris, Antwerp, Gant, *&c. than in any Ten Towns of the Reformation.* And is there more *charity* too? It doth not appear, if they be as ready to censure others, and admire themselves, as our Author, who so freely gives his Judgment about a matter it is impossible for him to know.

P. 77.
P. 79.
P. 81.
P. 82.
P. 83.

We see no reason to admire or imitate the manner of their Praying, and Fasting, and receiving the Sacraments; for *to pray without understanding, to fast without Abstinence, to receive a maimed Sacrament*, are things we do not envy them for; but altho our Devotion be not so pompous, and full of shew, yet We may pray and fast in secret, according to our Saviours Directions, far more than they do; however our People are mightily to blame if they do not understand what they pray for, if they do not receive more of the Sacrament than they; and we verily believe there are as great and remarkable Instances of *true Charity* among those of the Church of *England*, as among any People in the World.

XXXII. Of MIRACLES.

P. 83. 1. OUR Author saith, *He is not obliged to believe any one Miracle besides what is in Scripture.*

2. He sees no Reason to doubt *the truth of many Miracles, which are attested by great numbers of Eye witnesses, examined by Authority, and found upon Record, with all the Formalities due to such a Process.*

Now, how can these two things stand together? Is not a Man obliged to believe a thing so well proved? And if his other Arguments prove any thing, it is, that he is bound to believe them. For he thinks there is as much Reason to believe Miracles still, as in the time of the old or new Law. If he can make this out, I see no reason why he should not be as well obliged to believe them now, as those recorded in Scripture. But I can see nothing like a proof of this. And all Persons of Judgment in their own Church, do grant there is a great difference between the Necessity of Miracles for the first establishing a Religion, and afterwards. This is not only asserted by *Tostatus, Erasmus, Stella, Andradius*, and several others formerly;

Moyens Surs & Honestes. &c. To. 2. p. 49.

but the very late *French* Author I have several times mentioned, saith it in express Terms. And he confesses the great Impostures of modern Miracles, which, he saith, ought to be severely punished; and that none but Women and weak People think themselves bound to believe them. And he cannot understand what they

they are good for: Not to convert Hereticks; because not done among them: Not to prove there are no corruptions or errors among them, which is a thing incredible; with much more to that purpose, and so concludes with *Monsieur Paschal*, *That if they have no better use, we ought not to be amused with them.*

But *Christ* promised, *that his Apostles should do greater Miracles than himself had done.* And what then? Must therefore S. *Francis*, or S. *Dominic*, or S. *Rosa*, do as great as the Apostles had done? What Consequence can be drawn from the Apostles times to latter Ages? We do not dispute *God's Omnipotency, or say his hand is shortned*; but we must not from thence infer, that every thing which is called a Miracle is truly so; or make use of God's Power, to justifie the most incredible stories. VVhich is a way will serve as well for a false as a true Religion; and *Mahomet* might run to Gods Omnipotency for cleaving the Moon in two pieces, as well as others for removing a House over the Seas, or any thing of a like nature.

But, he saith, *their Miracles are not more ridiculous and absurd than some in the Old Testament.* Which I utterly deny; but I shall not run out into the examination of this Parallel, by shewing how very different the Nature, Design, and Authority of the Miracles he mentions, is from those which are believed in the *Roman* Church. And it had been but fitting, as he set down the Miracles of the *Old Testament*, so to have mentioned those of the *Roman* Church which were to vye with them; but this he was willing to forbear, for certain good Reasons. *If most of poor Man's impossibles be none to God,* as he concludes, yet every thing is not presently true which is not impossible; and by this way of Arguing, there can be nothing objected against the most absurd and idle Fictions of the Golden Legend, which all Men of Understanding among themselves, not only reject for want of Authority, but of Credibility.

XXXIII. Of Holy Water.

THE *Misrepresenter* charges him with *approving superstitious uses* of inanimate things, and attributing wonderful **effects** to them; as Holy Water, Candles, Oyl, Bread, &c.

In Answer, our Author 1. declares, *That the Papist truely represented, utterly disapproves all sorts of Superstition.* But if he had designed to have represented truely, he ought to have told us what he meant by Superstition, and whether any Man who observes the Commands of the Church can be guilty of it.

P. 86.

2. He saith, *That these things are particularly deputed by the Prayers and Blessing of the Priest to certain uses for God's Glory, and the Spiritual and Corporal Good of Christians.*

This is somewhat too general; but *Marsilius Columna*, Archbishop of *Salerno*, who hath taken most pains in this matter, sums them up; 1. As to Spiritual, they are Seven. 1. To fright Devils. 2. To remit Venial sins. 3. To cure Distractions 4. To elevate the Mind. 5. To dispose it for Devotion. 6. To obtain Grace. 7. To prepare for the Sacrament.

Hydragiolog. Sect. 3. c. 2. p. 45.

2. As to Corporal. 1. To cure Barrenness. 2. To multiply Goods. 3. To procure Health. 4. To purge the Air from pestilential Vapours.

And now, as our Author saith, *What Superstition in the use of it?* He names several things of Gods own appointing to Parallel it; as *the Waters of Jealousy, the Shew-bread, the Tables of Stone*; but the first was miraculous, the other had no such effects that we ever heard of. *Elisha's Salt for sweetning the Water*, was undoubtedly a Miracle. Is the *Holy-Water* so? As to the *Liver of the Fish for expelling the Devil*, in the Book of *Tobit*, he knows the Book is not owned for Canonical by us; and this very place is produced as an Argument against it; there being no Ground from Scripture, to attribute the Power of expelling Devils, to the Liver of a Fish, either naturally or symbolically: *Vallesius* offers at the only probable account of it, that it must be a Divine Power given to it, which the Angel *Raphael* did not discover; and yet it is somewhat hard to conceive, how this Liver should

V llef. Sacr. Iosoph. c. 58. p. 229.

should have such a power to drive away any kind of Devil, as it is there expressed, unless by a Devil there, no more be meant than some violent Disease, which the *Jews* generally believed to arise from the possession of evil Spirits: But however here is an Angel supposed, who made this known to *Tobit*; but we find not *Raphael* to discover the virtue of Holy Water against Devils. As to *Christ using Clay to open the Eyes of the Blind*, it is very improperly applied, unless the same miraculous Power be supposed in it, which was in Christ himself: And so is the *Apostles laying on of Hands, and using Oyl for miraculous Cures*; unless the same Gift of Miracles be in every Priest which consecrates Holy Water, which was in the Apostles: And *Bellarmine* himself confesses, *That no infallible effect doth follow the use of Holy Water, because there is no Promise of God in the case, but only the prayers of the Church. But these are sufficient to sanctifie the Water*, saith our Author: And to what end? For all the spiritual and corporeal benefits before mentioned? Is no promise of God necessary for such purposes as those? How can any Church in the World dispose of Gods Power without his Will? It may appoint significant and decent Ceremonies, but it can never appropriate Divine Effects to them; and to suppose any Divine Power in things which God never gave them, is in my Opinion, Superstition; and to use them for such ends, is a superstitious use. St *Cyril*, whom he quotes, speaks of the Consecration of the Water of Baptism, *Catech*. 3. St. *Augustine* only of a consecrated Bread, which the *Catechumens* had (*De Peccat. Merit. & Remiss.* l. 2. c. 26.) but he attributes no Divine Effects to it. Pope *Alexanders Epistle* is a notorious Counterfeit. Those Passages of *Epiphanius, Theodoret*, and S. *Jerom*, all speak of miraculous effects; and those who had the power of Miracles, might sometimes do them with an external sign, and sometimes without, as the Apostles cured with anointing, and without: But this is no ground for consecrating Oyl by the Church, or Holy Water, for miraculous Effects. If these Effects which they attribute to *Holy Water*, be miraculous, then every Priest must have not only a power of Miracles himself, but of annexing it to the Water he consecrates; if they be super-natural, but not miraculous, then Holy Water must be made a Sacrament to produce these Effects *ex opere operato*; if neither one nor the other, I know not how to excuse the use of it from *Superstition*.

De Cultu Sanct. l.3.c.7

XXXIV. Of breeding up People in Ignorance.

THe *Misrepresenter* charges them with this, on these Accounts. 1. By keeping their Mysteries of Iniquity from them. 2. By performing Divine Service in an unknown Tongue. 3. By an implicite Faith. To which the *Representer* answers. 1. *That they give encouragement to Learning*; and he instances *in their Universities and Conventual Libraries*; But what is all this to the common People? But their *Indices Expurgatorii*, *and prohibiting Books so severely*, which are not for their turn, (as we have lately seen in the new one of *Paris*) argues no great confidence of their Cause, nor any hearty love to Learning: And if it could be rooted out of the World, their Church would fare the better in it; but if it cannot, they must have some to be able to deal with others in it. 2. As to the common People he faith, *They have Books enough to instruct them*. Is it so in *Spain* or *Italy*? But where they live among Hereticks, as we are called, the People must be a little better instructed to defend themselves, and to gain upon others. 3. *If the People did know their Church-Offices and Service*, &c. *they would not find such faults, since the Learned approve them*. Let them then try the Experiment, and put the Bible and their Church-Offices every where into the Vulgar Tongues: But their severe Prohibitions shew how much they are of another Opinion: What made all that Rage in *France* against *Voisins* Translation of the *Missal*? Such Proceedings of the Assembly of the Clergy against it; such complaints both to the King and the Pope against it, as tho all were lost, if that were suffered? Such an Edict from the King, such a Prohibition from the Pope in such a Tragical Stile about it? Such a Collection of Authors to be printed on purpose against it? Do these things shew, even in a Nation of so free a Temper, in Comparison as the *French*, any mighty Inclination towards the encouraging this Knowledg in the People? And since that, what stirs have there been about the *Mons Testament*? What Prohibitions by Bishops? besides a Bull from this very Pope against it. What vehement Opposition by others? So that many Volumes have already been written on the occasion of that Translation. And yet our Author would perswade

P. 89.

P. 90.

Collectio Authorum Vulg. Versiones damnantium Jussu. ac Mandato Cleri Gallicani edita. Lutet. Paris. 1661.

perswade us, *That if we look abroad, we shall find wonderful care taken to keep the People from Ignorance*; but we can discern much greater to keep them in it.

XXXV. *Of the Uncharitableness of the Papists.*

THe *Misrepresenter*, (as he is called) charges this Point home, *Because they deny Salvation to those who believe all the Articles of the Christian Faith in the Apostles Creed, and lead vertuous and good Lives, if they be not of their Communion.*

To this the *Representer* answers in plain terms, *That this is nothing but what they have learnt from the mouth of Christ and his Apostles.* And to this end he musters up all their sayings against Infidels, false Apostles, *Gnosticks, Cerinthians*, as tho they were point-blank levelled against all that live out of the Communion of the Church of *Rome*.

But *this is no Uncharitableness, but pure zeal, and the same the Primitive Church shewed against Hereticks, such as* Marcior, Basilides, *and* Bardesanes, *who were condemned in the first Age for denying the Resurrection of the dead* &c. What in the first Age! Methinks the Second had been early enough for them: But this is to let us see what Learning there is among you. But do we deny the Resurrection of the Dead? Or hold any one of the Heresies condemned by the Primitive Church? What then is our Fault, which can merit so severe a Sentence? *We oppose the Church:* What Church? The Primitive Apostolical Church? The Church in the time of the four General Councils? I do not think that will be said, but I am sure it can never be proved: What Church then? *The present Church?* Is it then damnable to oppose the present Church? But I pray let us know what ye mean by it; *The Universal Body of Christians in the World?* No, No, abundance of them are *Hereticks and Schismaticks*, as well as we: *i. e.* All the Christians in the *Eastern* and *Southern* parts, who are not in Communion with the Church of *Rome:* So that two parts in three of Christians, are sent to Hell by this Principle; and yet it is no Uncharitableness. But suppose the Church of *Rome* be *the only true Church*, must men be damned

O 2 presently

presently for opposing its Doctrines? I pray think a little better on it, and you will change your Minds. Suppose a Man do not submit to the Guides of this Church in a matter of Doctrine declared by them; Must he be Damned? What if it be the Deposing Power? Yet his Principle is, *If a Man do not hold the Faith entire, he is gone.* But Popes and Councils have declared this to be a point of Faith; therefore if he doth not hold it, he must be damned. There is no way of answering this, but he must abate the severity of his Sentence against us. For upon the same Reason he questions that, we may question many more. And all his Arguments against us, will hold against himself; For, saith he, *he that disbelieves one Article of Catholick Faith, does in a manner disbelieve all.* Let him therefore look to it, as well as we. But he endeavours to prove *the Roman Catholick Church to be the true Church, by the ordinary Notes and Marks of the Church.* Although he is far enough from doing it; yet this will not do his business. For he must prove, that we are convinced that it is the true Church; and then indeed he may charge us with *Obstinate Opposition*, but not before. And it is a very strange thing to me, that when their Divines say, that Infidels shall not be damned for their Infidelity, where the Gospel hath not been sufficiently proposed to them; and no Christian for not believing any Article of Faith till it be so proposed; that we must be damned for not believing the Articles of the *Roman* Faith, which never have been, and never can be sufficiently proposed to us. Methinks such men should Study a little better their own Doctrine about the sufficient Proposal of matters of Faith, before they pass such uncharitable and unlearned Censures.

XXXVI. *Of Ceremonies and Ordinances.*

HIS Discourse on this Head is against those who refuse to obey their Superiours in things not expressed in Scripture, which is no part of our Controversy with them. But yet there are several things about their Ceremonies we are not satisfied in: As
1. The mighty Number of them, which have so much muffled up the Sacraments, that their true face cannot be discerned.
2. The Efficacy attributed to them, without any promise
from

rom God; whereas we own no more but decency and significancy. 3. The Doctrine that goes along with them, not only of Obedience, but of Merit; and some have asserted the *Opus Operatum* of Ceremonies as well as Sacraments, when the Power of the Keys goes along with them; *i. e.* when there hath been some Act of the Church exercised about the Matter of them; as in the Consecration of Oyl, Salt, Bread, Ashes, Water, &c.

XXXVII. *Of Innovation in matters of Faith.*

THe Substance of his Discourse on this Head may be reduced to these things. 1. *That the Church in every Age hath Power to declare what is necessary to be believed, with Anathema to those who Preach the Contrary; and so the Council of* Trent, *in declaring Transubstantiation, Purgatory,* &c. *to be necessary Articles, did no more than the Church had done before on like Occasions.* P. 108, 109.
2. *That if the Doctrines then defined had been Innovations, they must have met with great Opposition when they were introduced.* P. 112, &c:
3. *That those who charged those points to be Innovations, might as well have laid the scandal on any other Article of Faith which they retained.* P. 116.

These are things necessary to be examined, in order to the making good the charge of Innovation in matters of Faith, which we believe doth stand on very good Grounds.

1. We are to consider, Whether the Council of *Trent* had equal Reason to define the necessity of these points, as the Council of *Nice* and *Constantinople* had to determin the point of the Trinity; or those of *Ephesus* and *Chalcedon,* the Truth of Christ's Incarnation. He doth not assert it to be in the Churches Power to make new Articles of Faith, as they do imply new Doctrines revealed; but he contends earnestly, That the Church hath a Power to declare the necessity of believing some points which were not so declared before. And if the Necessity of believing doth depend upon the Churches Declaration, then he must assert, that it is in the Churches Power to make points necessary to be believed, which were not so; and consequently to make common Opinions to become Articles of Faith. But I hope we may have leave to enquire in this Case, since the Church pretends to no new Revelation of matters of Doctrine, therefore it can declare no more than
P. 109.

than it receives, and no otherwise than it receives. And so nothing can be made necessary to Salvation but what God himself hath made so by his Revelation. So that they must go in their Declaration either upon Scripture, or Universal Tradition; but if they define any Doctrine to be necessary without these Grounds, they exceed their Commission, and there is no Reason to submit to their Decrees, or to believe their Declarations. To make this more plain by a known Instance: It is most certain that several Popes and Councils have declared the Deposing Doctrine, and yet our Author saith, *It is no Article of Faith with him.* Why not, since the Popes and Councils have as evidently delivered it, as the Council of *Trent* hath done Purgatory, or Transubstantiation? But he may say, *There is no Anathema joined to it.* Suppose there be not; But why may it not be, as well as in the other Cases? And if it were, I would know, whether in his Conscience he would then believe it to be a necessary Article of Faith, tho he believed that it wanted Scripture and Tradition? If not, then he sees what this matter is brought to, *viz.* That altho the Council of *Trent* declare these new Doctrines to be necessary to be believed; yet if their Declaration be not built on Scripture and Universal Tradition, we are not bound to receive it.

2. *As to the impossibility of Innovations coming in without notorious opposition,* I see no ground at all for it, where the alteration is not made at once, but proceeds gradually. He may as well prove it impossible for a Man to fall into a *Dropsy* or a *Hectick-Fever*, unless he can tell the punctual time when it began. And he may as well argue thus, Such a Man fell into a Fever upon a great Debauch, and the Physicians were presently sent for to advise about him; therefore the other Man hath no Chronical Distemper, because he had no Physicians when he was first sick; as because Councils were called against some Heresies, and great Opposition made to them, therefore where there is not the like, there can be no *Innovation.* But I see no Reason why we should decline giving an Account, by what Degrees, and Steps, and upon what Occasions, and with what Opposition several of the Doctrines defined at *Trent* were brought in. For the matter is not so obscure as you would make it, as to most of the Points in difference between us. But that is too large a Task to be here undertaken.   3. There

3. There is no Colour for calling in Queſtion the Articles of Faith received by us on the ſame Grounds that we reject thoſe defined by the Council of *Trent*; for we have the Univerſal Conſent of the Chriſtian World for the Apoſtles Creed; and of the Four General Councils for the Doctrines of the Trinity and Incarnation; who never pretended to determine any Point to be neceſſary which was not revealed in Scripture; whoſe ſenſe was delivered down by the Teſtimony of the Chriſtian Church from the Apoſtles times. But the Council of *Trent* proceeded by a very different Rule; for it firſt ſet up *an Unwritten Word* to be a Rule of Faith, as ſeſſ. Quarta. well as *the Written*; which altho it were neceſſary in order to their Decrees, was one of the greateſt Innovations in the World; and the Foundation of all the reſt, as they were there eſtabliſhed.

An Anſwer to the *CONCLUSION*.

Having thus gone through the ſeveral Heads, which our Author complains have been ſo much *Miſrepreſented*; it is now fit to conſider what he ſaith in his *Concluſion*, which he makes to anſwer his *Introduction*, by renewing therein his doleful Complaints of their being *Miſrepreſented juſt as Chriſt and his Apoſtles, and the Primitive Chriſtians were.* I P 119. hope the former Diſcourſe hath ſhewed their Doctrines and Practices are not ſo very like thoſe of *Chriſt and his Apoſtles, and the Primitive Chriſtians*, that their Caſes ſhould be made ſo parallel: but as in his Concluſion he hath ſummed up the ſubſtance of his *Repreſentations*, ſo I ſhall therein follow his Method, only with this difference, that I ſhall in one Column ſet down his own *Repreſentations* of Popery, and in the other the Reaſons, in ſhort, why we cannot embrace them.

Wherein Popery conſiſts as Repreſented by this Author.	Our Reaſons againſt it in the ſeveral Particulars.
1. IN uſing all external Acts of Adoration before Images, as *Kneeling, Praying, lifting up the Eyes, burning Candles, Incenſe*, &c. Not merely to worſhip the Objects before them, but to worſhip the Images themſelves on the account of the Ob-	1. Thou ſhalt not make to thy ſelf any graven Image, or any likeneſs of any thing in Heaven, or Earth, &c. Thou ſhalt not bow down to them, nor worſhip them. Which being the plain clear, and expreſs Words of the Divine Law, we dare not worſhip any

Popery as Represented.	Our Reasons against it.

jects represented by them: or in his own Words, *Because the Honour that is exhibited to them, is referred to the Prototypes which they represent.* P. 3.

any Images, or Representations, lest we be found Transgressors of this Law. Especially since God herein hath declared himself a *Jealous God*; and annexed so severe a Sanction to it. And since he that made the Law is only to interpret it, all the Distinctions in the World can never satisfie a Mans Conscience, unless it appear that God himself did either make or approve them. And if God allow the Worship of the thing Represented by the Representation, he would never have forbidden that Worship absolutely, which is unlawful only in a certain respect.

2. *In joining the Saints in Heaven together with Christ in Intercession for us, and making Prayers on Earth to them on that Account.* P. 5.

2. *We have an Advocate with the Father, Jesus Christ the righteous,* 1 John 2. 1. *And one Mediator between God and Men, the Man Christ Jesus,* 1 Tim. 2. 5. *For Christ is entred into Heaven it self, now to appear in the Presence of God for us,* Heb. 9. 24. And therefore we dare not make other *Intercessors in Heaven* besides him: and the distance between Heaven and us, breaks off all Communication between the Saints there, and us upon Earth; so that all Addresses to them now for their Prayers, are in a way very different from desiring others on earth to pray for us: And if such Addresses are made in the solemn Offices of Divine Worship, they join the Creatures with the Creator in the Acts and Signs of Worship, which are due to God alone.

3. Call

Popery as Represented.	Our Reasons against it.
3. In allowing more Supplications to be used to the Blessed Virgin, than to Christ; For he denies it to be *an idle Superstition*, to repeat *Ten Ave Maria's* for one *Pater Noster*.	3. **Call** *upon me in the Day of Trouble, I will deliver thee, and thou shalt glorifie me*, Psal. 50. 15. When we pray to *Our Father in Heaven*, as our Saviour commanded us, we do but what both Natural and Christian Religion require us to do: But when men pray to the Blessed Virgin for *Help and Protection now, and at the Hour of Death*, they attribute that to her, which belongs only to God, who is our *Helper and Defender*: And altho Christ knew *the Dignity of his Mother* above all others, he never gives the least encouragement to make such Addresses to her: And to suppose her to have a share now in the Kingdom of Christ in Heaven, as a Copartner with him, is to advance a Creature to Divine Honour, and to overthrow the true Ground of Christs Exaltation to his Kingdom in Heaven, which was, His suffering on the Cross for us.
4. In giving Religious Honour and Respect to Relicks. Such as placing them upon Altars, burning Wax-Candles before them, carrying them in Processions, to be seen, touched, or humbly kissed by the People: Which are the known and allowed Practices in the Church of *Rome*. P. 8.	4. *And no man knoweth of the Sepulcher of Moses unto this day*, Deut. 34. 6. Why should God hide the Body of *Moses* from the People, if he allowed *giving Religious Honour and Respect to Relicks*? Why should *Hezekiah break in Pieces the Brazen Serpent, because the Children of Israel did burn Incense to it*? 2 Kings 18. 4. Especially when it was a Type or Representation of Christ himself, and God had wrought many Miracles by it.

| Popery as Represented. | Our Reasons against it. |

5. In adoring Christ as present in the Eucharist on the account of the Substance of Bread and Wine being changed into that Body of Christ which suffered on the Cross. P. 10.

5. Whom the Heaven must receive until the times of the Restitution of all things, Acts 3. 21. And therefore in the Eucharist we adore him, as *sitting on the right hand of God*; but we dare not direct our Adoration to the Consecrated Host, which we believe to be the Substance of Bread and Wine, (tho consecrated to a Divine Mystery), and therefore not a fit Object for our Adoration.

6. In believing the Substance of Bread and Wine by the Words of Consecration, to be changed into his own Body and Blood, the Species only or Accidents of Bread and Wine remaining as before. P. 10.

6. *The Bread which we break, is it not the Communion of the Body of Christ*, 1 Cor. 10. 16. This is spoken of the Bread after Consecration, and yet the Apostle supposes it to be Bread still, and the *Communion of his Body* is interpreted by the next Words, *For we being many, are one Bread, and one Body ; for we are all Partakers of that one Bread*, v 17. Which is very different from the Bread being changed into the very Body of Christ; which is an Opinion that hath no Foundation in Scripture, and is repugnant to the common Principles of Reason, which God hath given us, and exposes Christian Religion to the Reproach and Contempt of *Jews, Turks, and Infidels*.

7. In making good Works to be truly meritorious of Eternal Life. P. 13.

7. *When ye shall have done all those things which are commanded you, say, We are unprofitable servants, we have done that which was our duty to do*, St. Luke 17. 10. And therefore in no sense can our best Works be *truly Meritorious of Eternal Life:* Which consisting

Popery as Represented.	Our Reasons against it.
	sitting in the enjoyment of God, it is impossible there should be any just Proportion, or due Commensuration between our best Actions, and such a Reward.
8. In making Confession of our sins to a Priest in order to Absolution. P. 14.	8. *And the Son said unto him, Father I have sinned against Heaven, and in thy sight*, St. Luke 15. 21. Where Confession to God is required because the Offence is against him, but it is impossible for any Man upon earth to forgive those whom God doth not forgive: And he alone can appoint the necessary Conditions of Pardon, among which true Contrition and Repentance is fully declared; but *Confession to a Priest*, tho it may be useful for the ease of the Penitent, is no where in Scripture made necessary for the Forgiveness of Sin.
9. In the use of Indulgences for taking away the Temporal Punishments of sin, remaining due after the Guilt is remitted.	9. *I said, I will confess my Transgressions unto the Lord; and thou forgavest the iniquity of my sin*, Psal. 32. 5. If God doth fully forgive the *Guilt* of sin, there remains no Obligation to punishment; for whereever that is, the *guilt* remains: It is true, God may not sometimes fully pardon; but he may reserve some temporal punishment here for his own Honour, or the Chastisement of a penitent Sinner: But then what have any men to do, to pretend that they can take off what God thinks fit to lay on? Can any *Indulgences* prevent pain or Sickness, or sudden Death? But if *Indulgences* be understood only with respect

Popery as Represented.

10. *In supposing that Penitent Sinners may in some measure satisfy by Prayer, Fasting, Alms, &c. for the Temporal Pain, which by order of God's Justice sometimes remains due, after the Guilt and the Eternal Pain are remitted.* P. 17.

11. *In thinking the Scripture not fit to be read generally by all, without Licence, or in the Vulgar Tongues.* P. 19.

Our Reasons against it.

respect to *Canonical Penances*, they are a most notorious and inexcusable Corruption of the Discipline of the Ancient Church.

10. *For if when we were Enemies, we were reconciled to God by the death of his Son; much more, being reconciled, we shall be saved by his Life,* Rom. 5. 10. And therefore no Satisfaction to the Justice of God is now required from us, for the Expiation of any remainder of Guilt. For if Christ's Satisfaction were in it self sufficient for a total Remission, and was so accepted by God; what Account then remains for the Sinner to discharge, if he perform the Conditions on his part? But we do not take away hereby the Duties of *Mortification*, *Prayer*, *Fasting*, and *Alms*, &c. but there is a difference to be made between the *Acts* of *Christian Duties*, and *Satisfaction to Divine Justice* for the Guilt of Sin, either in whole or in part. And to think to joyn any Satisfactions of ours, together with Christs, is like joyning our hand with Gods in Creating or Governing the World.

11. *Let the Word of Christ dwell in you richly in all Wisdom; teaching and admonishing one another,* &c. Coloss. 3. 16.

How could that *dwell richly in them*, which was not to be communicated to them, but with great Caution? How could *they teach and admonish*

Popery as Represented.	Our Reasons against it.
	monish one another in a Language not understood by them? The Scriptures of the *New Testament* were very early perverted; and if this Reason were sufficient to keep them out of the Hands of the People, certainly they would never have been published for common use, but as prudently dispensed then, as some think it necessary they should be now. But we esteem it a part of our Duty, not to think our selves wiser than Christ or his Apostles, nor to deprive them of that unvaluable Treasure which our Saviour hath left to their use.
12. In allowing the Books of Tobit, Judith, Ecclesiasticus, Wisdom, Maccabees, to be Canonical, P. 21.	12. *All Scripture is given by Inspiration of God*, 2 Tim. 3. 16. *Holy men of God spake as they were moved by the Holy-Ghost*, 2 Pet. 1. 21. Therefore, where there is no Evidence of Divine Inspiration, those Books cannot be made Canonical. But the Jewish Church, *To whom the Oracles of God were committed*, never deliver'd these Books as any part of them, being Written when Inspiration was ceased among them. And it is impossible for any Church in the World to make that to be divinely inspired, which was not so from the beginning.
13. In preferring the Vulgar Latin Edition of the Bible before any other, and not allowing any Translations into a Mother Tongue to be ordinarily read. P. 24. 26.	13. But I say, *Have they not heard? Yes verily, their sound went into all the Earth, and their Words unto the ends of the World*. Rom. 10. 18. Therefore the Intention of God was, that the Gospel should be under-

Popery as Represented.	Our Reasons against it.

stood by all Mankind; which it could never be, unless it were translated into their several Languages. But still the difference is to be observed, between the Originals and Translations; and no Church can make a *Translation* equal to the *Original*. But among Translations, those deserve the greatest esteem which are done with the greatest Fidelity and Exactness. On which account our last Translation deserves a more particular Regard by us; as being far more useful to our People, than the *Vulgar Latin*, or any Translation made only from it.

14. In believing that the Scripture alone can be no Rule of Faith to any Private or particular Person. P. 28.

14. *Thy Word is a Lamp unto my Feet, and a Light unto my Path,* Psalm 119. 105.

Which it could never be, unless it were sufficient for necessary direction in our way to Heaven. But we suppose Persons to make use of the best means for understanding it, and to be duely qualified for following its Directions: without which, the best Rule in the World can never attain its End. And if the Scripture have all the due Properties of a Rule of Faith, it is unconceivable why it should be denied to be so; unless men find they cannot justify their Doctrines and Practices by it, and therefore are forced to make Tradition equal in Authority with it.

15. In relying upon the Authority of the present Church for the Sense of Scripture. P. 29.

15. *Wo unto you Lawyers, for ye have taken away the Key of Knowledg; ye*

Popery as Represented.	Our Reasons against it.
	ye entred not in your selves, and them that were entring in, ye hindred. S. Luk. 11. 52.
	From whence it follows, that the present Guides of the Church may be so far from giving the true Sense of Scripture, that they may be the chief Means to hinder Men from right understanding it. Which argument is of greater force, because those who plead for the Infallibility of the Guides of the present Church, do urge the promises made to the Jewish Church at that time; as our Author doth from those *who sat in the Chair of* Moses, *and from* Caiaphas *his Prophesying.*
16. *In receiving and believing the Churches Traditions as the Doctrine of Christ and his Apostles, and assenting to them with Divine Faith, just as he doth to the* Bible. P. 31, 32.	16. *We have also a more sure word of Prophesie; whereunto ye do well that ye take heed,* 2 Pet. 1. 19. And yet here the Apostle speaks of something delivered by the Testimony of those who were with Christ in the Holy Mount. From whence we infer, that it was not the Design of Christ to leave us to any *Vocal Testimony,* but to refer us to the *Written word,* as the most certain Foundation of Faith. And it is not any Persons assuming the Title of the Catholick Church to themselves, can give them Authority to impose any Traditions on the Faith of Christians; or require them to be believed, equally with the Written Word. For before any Traditions can be assented to with Divine Faith, the Churches Autho-

Popery as Represented.	Our Reasons against it.
	Authority must be proved to be Divine and Infallible, either by a written or unwritten Word; but it can be done by neither, without overthrowing the necessity of such an Infallibility in order to Divine Faith; because the Testimony on which the Churches Infallibility is proved, must be received only in a way of Credibility.
17. In believing that the Present Guides of the Church being assembled in Councils for preserving the Unity of the Church, have an Infallible Assistance in their Decrees. P. 38.	17. *Also of your own selves shall Men arise, speaking perverse things to draw away Disciples after them*, Acts 20.30. Which being spoken of the *Guides* of the *Christian Church*, without Limitation of Number, a possibility of Error is implied in any Assembly of them; unless there were some other Promises which did assure us, That in all great Assemblies the Spirit of God shall always go with the casting Voice, or the greater Number.
18. In believing the Pope to be the Supreme head of the Church under Christ, being Successor to S. Peter to whom he committed the care of his Flock. P. 40, 41.	18. *And he gave some Apostles, and some Prophets, and some Evangelists, and some Pastors and Teachers——for the edifying of the Body of Christ——till we all come in the Unity of the Faith*, &c. Ephes. 4. 13, 14, 15. Now here being an account given of the Officers Christ appointed in his Church, in order to the *Unity* and *Edification* of it, it had been unfaithfulness in the Apostle to have left out the Head of it, in case Christ had appointed any. Because this were of more consequence than all the rest; being declared necessary to Salvation

Popery as Represented.	Our Reasons against it.
	Salvation to be in subjection to him. But neither this Apostle, nor S. *Peter* himself, give the least intimation of it. Which it is impossible to conceive should have been left out in the Apostolical writings upon so many occasions of mentioning it, if ever Christ had instituted a Headship in the Church, and given it to S. *Peter* and his Successors in the See of *Rome*.
19. *In believing that Communion in both Kinds is an indifferent thing; and was so held for the first four hundred years after Christ; and that the first Precept for Receiving under both Kinds, was given to the Faithful by Pope* Leo I. *and confirmed by Pope* Gelasius. P. 51.	19. *For as often as ye eat this Bread, and drink this Cup, ye do shew the Lord's death till he come*, 1 Cor. 15. 26. The Apostle speaking to all Communicants, plainly shews, that the Institution of Christ was, That all should partake of both Kinds, and so to continue to do as long as this Sacrament was to shew forth the Death of Christ, *viz.* till his Second coming. And there is no colour for asserting the Christian Church ever looked on observing Christs Institution in this matter as an indifferent thing; no not for a thousand years after Christ. Altho the Practice and the Obligation are two things, yet when the Practise was so agreeable to the Institution, and continued so long in the Church; it is hardly possible for us to prove the sense of the Obligation, by a better way than by the continuance of the Practise. And if some Traditions must be thought binding, and far from being indifferent, which want all that Evidence which this practise carries along with it, How unreasonable is it in this Case to allow the Practise, and to deny the Obligation?

Popery as Represented.	Our Reasons against it.
20. In believing that the Doctrine of Purgatory is founded on Scripture, Authority, and Reason. P. 54, &c.	20. *And whom he justified, them he also glorified*, Rom. 8. 30. But whom God justifies, they have the Remission of their Sins as to Eternal Punishment. And if those who are thus justified, must be glorified, what place is there for Purgatory? For there is not the least intimation of any other state of Punishment that any who are justified must pass through before they are admitted to Glory. We grant they may, notwithstanding, pass through many intermediate trials in this World; but we say, where there is Justification, there is *no Condemnation*; but where any part of guilt remains unremitted, there is a Condemnation remaining so far as the punishment extends. And so this distinction as to Eternal and Temporal Pains, as it is made the Foundation of Purgatory, is wholly groundless; and therefore the Doctrine built upon it can have no Foundation in Scripture or Reason.
21. In believing that to the saying of Prayers well and devoutly, it is not necessary to have attention on the Words, or on the Sense of Prayers. P. 62.	21. *I will pray with the Spirit, and I will pray with the Understanding also*, 1 Cor. 14. 15. What need *this Praying with the Understanding*, if there were no necessity of attending to the sense of Prayers? For then *praying with the Spirit* were all that was required: For that supposes *an attention of the Mind upon God*. And I can hardly believe any Man that thinks with understanding, can justifie praying without it: Especially when there are Exhortations and

Popery as Represented.	Our Reasons against it.
	and Invitations to the People to joyn in those Prayers, as it is plain there are in the *Roman* Offices.
22. In believing that none out of the Communion of the Church of Rome can be saved; and that it is no Uncharitableness to think so. P. 92.	22. *Then Peter opened his mouth, and said, Of a truth I perceive that God is no respecter of Persons; but in every Nation, he that feareth God, and worketh Righteousness, is accepted with him,* Acts 10. 34, 35. Whereby we perceive, that God doth not limit the possibility of Salvation under the Gospel to Communion with the See of *Rome*; for if S. *Peter* may be believed, the capacity of Salvation depends upon Mens *fearing God and working Righteousness*; and it is horrible Uncharitableness to exclude those from a possibility of Salvation, whom God doth not exclude from it.
23. In believing that the Church of Rome, *in all the new Articles defined at* Trent, *hath made no Innovation in matters of Faith.* P. 107.	23. *That ye should earnestly contend for the Faith which was once delivered to the Saints*, Jude v. 3. Therefore all necessary Doctrines of Faith were at first delivered; and whatever Articles cannot be proved to have been delivered by the Apostles, can never be made necessary to be believed in order to Salvation. Which overthrows the additional Creed of *Pius* IV. after the Council of *Trent*; and puts them upon the necessity of proving the Universal Tradition of those Doctrines from the Apostolical Times: And when they do that, we may think better of them than at present we do; for as yet we can see neither *Scripture*, nor *Reason*, nor *Antiquity* for them.

Thus

THUS I have *Represented* that kind of *Popery* which our Author, (who complains so much of *Misrepresenting*) allows; and I have in short, set down how little ground we have to be fond of it; nay, to speak more plainly, it is that we can never yield to, without betraying the Truth, renouncing our Senses and Reason, wounding our Consciences, dishonouring God and his Holy Word and Sacraments, perverting the Doctrine of the Gospel as to Chrifts Satisfaction, Intercession and Remission of Sins; depriving the People of the Means of Salvation which God himself hath appointed, and the Primitive Church observed, and damning those for whom Christ died.

We do now in the sincerity of our Hearts appeal to God and the World, That we have no design to *Misreprefent* them, or to make their Doctrines and Practises appear worse than they are: But take them with all the Advantages even this Author hath set them out with, we dare appeal to the Judgments and Consciences of any impartial men, whether (the Scripture being allowed on both sides) our Doctrines be not far more agreeable thereto than the *new Articles* of *Trent*, which are the very Life and Soul of Popery? Whether our Worship of God be not more suitable to the Divine Nature and Perfections, and the Manifestations of his Will, than the *worship of Images*, and *Invocation of Fellow-Creatures*? Whether the plain Doctrine of the necessity of Repentance and sincere Obedience to the commands of Christ, do not tend more to promote Holiness in the World, than *the Sacrament of Penance*, as it is delivered and allowed to be practised in the Church of *Rome*, i. e. with the *easiness* and *efficacy* of *Absolution*, and getting off the remainders by *Indulgences*, *Satisfactions* of others, and *Prayers for the dead*? Whether it be not more according to the Institution of Christ to have *the Communion in both Kinds*, and to have *Prayers and the Scriptures in a Language which the People understand*? And lastly, whether there be not more of *Christian charity* in believing and hoping the best of those vast Bodies of Christians, who live out of the Communion of the Church of *Rome*, in the *Eastern, Southern, Western,* and *Northern* Parts, than to pronounce them all uncapable of Salvation on that Account? And therefore out of regard to God and the Holy Religion of our Blessed Saviour; out of regard to the Salvation of our own and other Souls, we cannot but very much prefer the Communion of our own Church, before that of the *Church* of *Rome*.

But before I conclude all, I must take some notice of his *Anathema's*: And here I am as much unsatisfied, as in any other part of his Book, and that for these Reasons.

1. Because he hath no manner of Authority to make them, suppose they were

were meant never so sincerely: And if we should ever object them to any others of that Church, they would presently say, *What had he to do to make Anathema's? It belongs only to the Church and the General Councils to pronounce Anathema's, and not to any private Person whatsoever.* So that if he would have published *Anathema's* with Authority, he ought to have printed those of the Council of *Trent*; *viz.* such as these,

Cursed is he that doth not allow the Worship of Images.
Cursed is he that saith Saints are not to be Invocated.
Cursed is he that doth not believe Transubstantiation, Purgatory, &c.

2. Because he leaves out an *Anathema* in a very material point, *viz. As to the Deposing Doctrine.* We do freely, and from our Hearts *Anathematize* all such Doctrines as tend to dissolve the Bonds of Allegiance to our Soveraign, on any pretence whatsoever. Why was this past over by him, without any kind of *Anathema*? Since he seems to approve the *Oxford Censures*, P. 48. Why did he not here show his zeal against all such dangerous Doctrines? *If the Deposing Doctrine* be falsly charged upon their Church, let us but once see it *Anathematized* by publick Authority of their Church, and we have done: But instead thereof, we find in a Book very lately published with great Approbations, by a present *Professor* at *Lovain Fr. D'Enghien,* all the Censures on the other side censured and despised, and the holding the Negative as to the *Deposing Doctrine,* is declared by him to be *Heresie, or next to Heresie:* The Censure of the *Sorbon* against *Sanctarellus,* he saith, *was only done by a Faction*; *and that of Sixty Eight Doctors, there were but Eighteen Present*; *and the late Censure of the* Sorbon, he saith, *was condemned by the Inquisition at* Toledo, Jan. 10. 1683. *as erroneous and Schismatical*; and so by the *Clergy* of *Hungary,* Oct. 24. 1682.

Auctoritas Sedis Apostolicæ in Reges, p. 374. 408. ad 430.

P. 549.

We do not question but there are Divines that oppose it; but we fear there are too many who do not; and we find they boast of their own numbers, and despise the rest as an inconsiderable Party: This we do not *Misrepresent* them in, for their most approved Books do shew it.

However, we do not question, but there are several worthy and Loyal Gentlemen of that Religion, of *different Principles and Practises*: And it is pity such be not distinguished from those who will not renounce a Doctrine so dangerous in the Consequences of it.

3. Because the *Anathema's* he hath set down, are not Penned so plainly and clearly, as to give any real Satisfaction: but with so much Art and Sophistry, as if they were intended to beguile weak and unwary Readers, who see not into the depth of these things, and therefore may think he hath done great

matters

matters in his *Anathema's*, when if they be strictly examined, they come to little or nothing; as

1. *Cursed is he that commits Idolatry.* An unwary Reader would think herein he disowned all that he accuses of *Idolatry*; but he doth not curse any thing as *Idolatry*, but what *himself* thinks to be so. So again, *Cursed is he* (not that gives Divine Worship to Images, but) *that prays to Images, or Relicks as Gods, or Worships them for Gods.* So that if he doth not take the Images themselves for Gods, he is safe enough from his own *Anathema*.

2. *Cursed is every goddess worshipper*, i. e. That believes the Blessed Virgin not to be a Creature. And so they escape all the force of this *Anathema*. *Cursed is he that Honours her, or puts his trust in her more than in God.* So that if they Honour her and trust in her but just as much as in God, they are safe enough; *Or that believes her to be above her Son:* But no *Anathema* to such as suppose her to be equal to him.

3. *Cursed is he that believes the Saints in Heaven to be his Redeemers, that prays to them as such.* What if men pray to them as their *Spiritual Guardians and Protectors*? Is not this giving Gods Honour to them? Doth this deserve no *Anathema*?

4. *Cursed is he that worships any breaden God, or makes Gods of the empty Elements of Bread and Wine:* viz. That supposes them to be *nothing but Bread and Wine*, and yet supposes them to be *Gods* too. Doth not this look like nonsense? And yet I am afraid our Author would think it a severe *Anathema* in this matter, to say, *Cursed is he who believes Nonsense and Contradictions.*

It will be needless to set down more, since I have endeavoured by clear stating the several Controversies, to prevent the Readers being imposed upon by deceitful *Anathema's*. And yet after all he saith,

Cursed are we, if in answering and saying Amen *to any of these Curses, we use any Equivocations or Mental Reservations, or do not assent to them in the common and obvious use of the Words.*

But there may be no Equivocation in the very Words, and yet there may be a great one in the intention and design of them: There may be none in saying *Amen* to the Curses so worded; but if he would have prevented all suspicion of Equivocation, he ought to have put it thus,

Cursed are we if we have not fairly and ingenuously expressed the whole Meaning of our Church as to the Points condemned in these Anathema's; or if we have by them designed to deceive the People: And then I doubt he would not so readily have said *Amen*.

THE

THE CONTENTS.

AN *Answer to his Introduction.* Page 1.
1. Of *Praying to Images.* p. 10.
2. Of *Worshipping Saints.* p. 17.
3. Of *Addressing more Supplications to the Virgin* Mary *than to Christ.* } p. 24.
4. Of *Paying Divine Worship to Relicks.* p. 30.
5. Of *the Eucharist.* p. 32.
   1. Of *Adoration of the Host.* p. 33.
   2. Of *Transubstantiation.* p. 35.
6. Of *Merits and good Works.* p. 42.
7. Of *Confession.* p. 46.
8. Of *Indulgences.* p. 48.
9. Of *Satisfaction.* p. 51.
10. Of *Reading the Holy Scriptures.* p. 52.
11. Of *Apocryphal Books* p. 55.
12. Of *the Vulgar Edition of the Bible.* p. 57.
13. Of *the Scripture as a Rule of Faith.* p. 58.
14. Of *the Interpretation of Scripture.* p. 59.
15. Of *Tradition.* p. 61.
16. Of *Councils.* p. 62.
17. Of *Infallibility in the Church.* p. 63.
18. Of *the Pope.* p. 65.
19. Of *Dispensations.* p. 68.
20. Of *the Deposing Power.* p. 71.
21. Of *Communion in one Kind.* p. 76.
22. Of *the Mass.* p. 79.
23. Of *Purgatory.* p. 80.
24. Of *Praying in an Unknown Tongue.* p. 86.

25. Of

25. Of the Second Commandment.	p. 88.
26. Of Mental Reservations.	p. 89.
27. Of a Deathbed Repentance.	p. 91.
28. Of Fasting.	p. 92.
29. Of Schisms and Divisions in the Church.	p. 94.
30. Of Friars and Nuns.	p. 96.
31. Of Wicked Principles and Practices.	p. 97.
32. Of Miracles.	p. 98.
33. Of Holy Water.	p. 100.
34. Of Breeding up People in Ignorance.	p. 102.
35. Of the Uncharitableness of the Papists.	p. 103.
36. Of Ceremonies and Ordinances.	p. 104.
37. Of Innovations in matters of Faith.	p. 105.
An Answer to his Conclusion.	p. 107.

FINIS.

ADVERTISEMENT.

A Discourse against Transubstantiation, Printed for *W. Rogers.*

www.ingramcontent.com/pod-product-compliance
Lightning Source LLC
Chambersburg PA
CBHW030403170426
43202CB00010B/1466